THE CONSCIOUS EDUCATOR

Becoming Culturally Responsive Teachers and Schools

Simone,

Thank you for your support!
Let's keep planting the seeds of
change!

-♡-

Sala S.

THE CONSCIOUS EDUCATOR

Becoming Culturally Responsive Teachers and Schools

BY

SALANDRA GRICE

www.bookstandpublishing.com

Published by
Bookstand Publishing
Morgan Hill, CA 95037
4723_3

ISBN 978-1-63498-851-3

"The paradox of education is this — that as one begins to become conscious, one begins to examine the society in which he is being educated in."

–James Baldwin

DEDICATION

I must first give thanks to the Lord Jesus Christ for His grace and mercy in my life. I could not have completed this book without the peace, comfort, and strength that can only come from Him. Glory be to God!

I am also thankful for the blessing of my wonderful husband, James. Without his support and sacrifice, I could not have journeyed down this road.

Thank you to my parents, Delores, Cedric, and Webster, for their unwavering support and encouragement. I thank them for always listening. I thank them for all of their love.

Thank you to my grandmother, Catherine Rogers, for all of her prayers.

Finally, this book is for my children, Layla and Cameron. I could not allow them to go through this world, leaving it as it is. I had to be the change and attempt to create the world I want for them. I pray they always love God, love themselves, and love others. I pray that they will always know that they can do anything in Christ.

ACKNOWLEDGEMENTS

This book was many years in the making, although I did not know it. Every moment, experience, success, and failure have all shaped the making of this project. There is a purpose in our pain. Although I could not write about every experience in this piece alone, many people throughout my life have helped make all this possible.

Thank you, Fred Wilson, for your mentorship and words of wisdom.

Thank you to everyone who helped during this writing process: Jo Ann Robisheaux, and Cedric Gilmore.

Thank you to my editor, Jamie Mayes, for all your guidance and support.

Thank you to Sara Pettit. Your kind words are forever in my heart.

Thank you Monica, Manuela, Sheila, and Mary. Your friendships mean the world to me.

Finally, thank you to everyone who ever told me what I couldn't do; it only made me want to do it more.

TABLE OF CONTENTS

Dedication vii

Acknowledgements viii

Foreword xi

Introduction: How Did We Get Here? xix

Chapter 1: Developing a Critical Consciousness 1

    Self-Reflection is Key 2
    The Basics of Diversity 8
    The Basics of Race 12
    What is Racism? 17
    What is Bias? 19
    What is Privilege? 22
    Intersectionality 24

Chapter 2: To See or Not to See 27

    What is Color Blindness? 27
    The Myth of Color Blindness 29
    The Pitfalls of Color Blindness 30
    From Color Blind to Color Conscious 33

Chapter 3: Culturally Responsive Teaching 37

    What is Culturally Responsive Teaching? 38
    What is Culture? 40
    A People's History Approach to Student Diversity 46
    Filling in the Gaps 48
    Poor and Low Income 58

Chapter 4: The Culturally Caring Classroom 65

    Actions Speak Louder than Nice Words 69
    Replacing Punitive Discipline Practices 74
    Different, Not Less 77
    Caring in Action 78
    Where is the Love? 81

Chapter 5: Creating Culturally Relevant Curriculums 83

    To Tell the Truth 83
    Whose History is it Anyway? 87
    Moving Forward 89
    What About the White Kids? 94
    Culturally Responsive Teaching is Effective Teaching 95
    The Framework 97

Afterword: Embracing the Challenge 101

References 105

About the Author 115

FOREWORD

"Education is the most powerful weapon which you can use to change the world."

–Nelson Mandela

I was a teacher, a kindergarten teacher to be exact. I spent nine years in the kindergarten classroom, and I loved every minute of it. I loved meeting new students every year. I loved seeing their little faces light up over smelly stickers, stinky feet passes, and extra center time. I loved teaching them the foundational skills needed to help them throughout their educational careers. The joys of watching them learn and grow from non-readers and writers to authors, mathematicians, scientists, historians, and good friends run deep within my heart.

It is because of my love for teaching and students that I have been brought to this critical point in my teaching career. I have come to a place where I can no longer stand by and do nothing. I cannot passively watch as the students I love are not being given the best learning opportunities to help them grow and develop. I have arrived at the point where I can no longer sit and watch students treated in less than desirable ways. These ways devalue their personhood and restrict their educational opportunities; and then it is these students who are blamed when they do not perform at high levels of achievement. I am past the point of silent compliance around discriminatory and harmful teaching practices. It is time for me to speak up and speak out.

Year after year, I watched, whispered, complained, and sometimes confronted the unequal and discriminatory practices within my schools. As a novice teacher, I did not always possess the patience to endure the ignorance and indifference that surrounded me. I was not always equipped with the language to articulate the educational wrongs that I witnessed. All I knew was that something had to change. Unsatisfied with the misinformed attempts made at my schools in addressing the most pressing issues our students face, I began a quest on my own. Now, armed with the promises from the theory, research, and practice of more effective instruction for diverse learners; I must share them with fellow teachers at large.

In a profession where the majority of the educators are from backgrounds vastly different from those of the students in their care, misunderstandings that stem from cultural differences between teachers and students can happen. The lack of understanding of how these cultural conflicts play an essential role in the quality of learning experiences for all students is the focus of this book. Deliberate focus and attention are made to point out that when well-intentioned teachers lack the tools necessary to help diverse students flourish, such can send students on a downward spiral of academic failures and disappointments. Teachers will come to understand that, as our classrooms become increasingly diverse, there is a need to help equip all teachers with the knowledge and skills necessary to nurture every student in their classrooms. I hope that this book will be the educator's new inspiration for more effective teaching in our 21st-century multiracial schools.

Becoming a teacher who is sensitive to the complex needs of diverse students is essential to creating equitable learning environments. By guiding teachers towards an increased knowledge in culturally responsive practices, I hope to reduce the cultural conflicts we are currently seeing in the classroom today. I want to begin to put an end to the negative statistics facing our culturally and linguistically diverse students in educational settings. Helping teachers abandon archaic teaching practices that stem from hegemonic traditions, fear, ignorance, and bias is essential in making room for more inclusive practices rooted in critical thinking, empathy, compassion, empowerment, understanding, acceptance, and love.

Is this a book about bashing teachers and placing the blame of student failure at the feet of educators? No. Is this a book about what a great teacher I am and how you can be the perfect teacher if you only become just like me? Absolutely not. Teaching is hard, and I am not perfect at it. As I look back throughout my teaching career, I can pinpoint numerous times when my lack of knowledge about more culturally responsive teaching practices resulted in perpetuating inequalities that were detrimental to the educational success of my diverse students. Did I intend to use less than effective teaching practices to instruct my diverse students? No. Unfortunately, good intentions are no excuse for continuing to engage in ineffective instructional practices when better alternatives are available. We must follow our good intentions with even better actions. In pointing out the blind spots in our deeply held beliefs about what "good teaching" is, I hope to open the door to conversations surrounding practices that promise to help us grow in our understanding of our diverse students and implement teaching practices that are more responsive to their needs. Teachers need knowledge of the diverse cultures, histories, experiences, perspectives, values, and beliefs of the culturally diverse students in their classes. Teachers need the knowledge of research and best practice of pedagogies in critical theories (Slattery, 2013). Teachers need to reflect on their level of socio-political consciousness around the issues our students face. This book will point teachers in the direction of attaining these critical foundational understandings.

I wrote this book with the knowledge that even though we have made significant gains in educational equality for all students, our public schools still struggle against the espoused ideas of equity in education by continuing to hold onto many centuries-old, unequal educational practices. When school districts across the nation continue to suffer from unequal funding, unequal access to quality curriculums, poor-quality teachers, segregated schooling, disparaging racial achievement gaps, and discipline rates, I would not be doing any favors by glossing over these harsh realities and the misinformed practices and beliefs that perpetuate them (Galster, 2012). They must be addressed and reformed.

Throughout these pages I will share scholarly research, educational best practices, and my personal teaching experiences to illustrate how even though our nation's educational system has come a long way in living up to its *Brown v. Board of Education (1954)* promises of an equal and quality education for all students; a critical examination of U.S. educational practices today paints a hard picture that's tough to reconcile as anything that defines equal (Tutwiler, 2007; Galster, 2012). As long as our most marginalized students still lack opportunities to receive high-quality educational experiences in spite of past historical victories, reform efforts will remain necessary, and strict conversations need to be held.

In this book, I will address our most pressing educational dilemmas, and provide teachers with the knowledge and tools to solve them. This book will reveal the need for more authentic and caring relationships between teachers and students. It will advocate for more culturally relevant curriculums, and provide teachers with the background knowledge and resources to help integrate such curriculums. It will address the need for teachers to become more aware of the challenges many of our culturally, linguistically, and economically diverse students face, and provide teachers with the tools to help these students overcome these challenges.

This book is designed to help equip every teacher with the ability to build authentic relationships and provide relevant and high-quality learning experiences for every student. This book seeks to change the current trend of lack of awareness of who students are, where they come from, and what they need. Ultimately, this book seeks to grow, inspire, challenge, and transform teachers to be better equipped to meet the needs of every student.

In a nation that is becoming more linguistically and ethnically diverse, there is a need to address the fact that such diversity is not reflected in public school educators. Lingering at 80 percent, those in charge of educating the most vulnerable and diverse students continue to remain White, middle-class, monolingual, and female (Miller, 2018). Because we still live in a society wrought with racial, gender, and class inequality, a particular mind shift or consciousness is needed by educators to ensure that the inequalities of our world are not replicated in our classrooms. However, none of the issues that stem from this reality can be addressed until we can first acknowledge the potential problems to which these demographic disparities contribute.

Although there are many unequal educational practices still perpetuated in public schools that often intersect with race, gender, and class, the focus of this book will be on the impact of race and culture in the classroom. There will be a particular focus on how the lack of knowledge on behalf of teachers in matters of race and culture impacts the classroom. As a result, I will be addressing some critical underlying racial themes, definitions, and terms in order to make sure teachers are all on the same page throughout the book. As educators, I believe we must be at the forefront of knowledge in the issues our students face. Educators having a shared understanding of their intended goals in obtaining racial equity in schools are vital in that process. Therefore, we must have a common understanding of the complexities and dynamics of race in this country so that we may have a better understanding of how race operates in our schools.

My hope in writing this book is that, through the examination of the state of public schools, the lessons learned throughout my teaching career, and the promises of culturally responsive teaching, more teachers will become conscious of the challenges still facing educational institutions. I look forward to more educators adopting the characteristics teachers need to help interrupt and eradicate educational practices that are not in the best interest of all students. I also hope that all the negative statistics facing schools regarding achievement gaps, discipline rates, and overall student success will begin to shift as our mindsets begin to shift in addressing our most pressing educational concerns. This shift in our mindsets towards the issues that our most marginalized students face isn't something that needs the approval of a legislature or school board, only a willingness to try. If we genuinely want to see positive changes in our schools, see all children succeed, and make the world a better place, then teachers must first begin to create the change within themselves.

The change needed for this kind of work will not only require a change of mind, but in many cases a change of heart as well. Developing the mindset necessary for this kind of work is essential, even critical, to becoming a more conscious educator. This critical consciousness, a term developed by Brazilian educator and activist Paulo Freire, serves as the catalyst in identifying and overturning harmful educational practices (Freire, 1974). He describes it in *Education for Critical Consciousness* (1974) as:

> *"...depth in the interpretation of problems; by the substitution of casual principles for magical explanations; by the testing of one's 'findings' and by openness to revision."* (p.15.)

Obtaining this critical consciousness allows individuals to become aware of the systems and institutions that they are part of, and to identify how these systems play a role in placing at a disadvantage or advantage those who live within its confines (Freire, 1974). In the context of our schools, conscious educators will be able to critically reflect on the schools in which they teach, and evaluate them for equity and equality. In becoming a critically conscious educator, one will no longer be satisfied with teaching practices that reinforce and maintain the status quo. Instead, conscious educators will be continuously critiquing the schools and school systems they are in by identifying potentially oppressive practices, and working to eliminate them and replace them with more emancipatory solutions. Conscious educators are change agents. Becoming a conscious educator is not another band-aid to cover up the problems in education; it is a revolution.

At times, the tone of this book may be uncomfortable. Believe me, as I am typing in words, my fingers are tempted to hit "Delete." However, I no longer can live in fear of what others may say. I can no longer live in fear of what others may think. If we truly believe the truth sets us free, then we must be open to the knowledge that frees us to be able to reach all students. Amid this freedom, we will finally be able to let go of convenient untruths that keep us from making real educational progress. In this freedom, we will become the most effective teachers, teachers able to meet the needs of our culturally, linguistically, ethnically, and economically diverse students.

The mission of this book is to inspire change by transforming our minds and motivating our hearts to act. As an experienced educator, I know that change is a big challenge for many who have been called to teach. We are, after all, creatures of habit (and convenience). However, if we are serious about the education and achievement of all students, we must begin to reconsider how we think about our students and what they are capable of accomplishing. If we are genuinely committed to equipping all students with the skills needed to succeed in this life, we must understand what barriers keep many of our students from achieving their goals — even if the barrier is us.

In becoming more conscious educators, we must come to grips with many of this book's revelations. This book will challenge teachers to rethink the mindset that our only obligations are to "treat all students the same," be kind, and teach the standards. However, this book will not only challenge teachers, but it will also give them hope. I hope that even amongst all the demands and responsibilities teachers face, we are still able to help in even the most troubling situations. This book seeks to be a light in the sometimes darkness of public school education. It seeks to help teachers correct many current educational wrongs. I am hopeful that once educators are made aware of the obstacles we still face, we will be inspired to overcome them. Maybe, once educators are presented with an alternative perspective on increasing student achievement, that new perspective will be embraced. I hope that once teachers know better, they will seek to do better. I hope.

INTRODUCTION

HOW DID WE GET HERE?

"Not everything that is faced can be changed. But nothing can be changed until it is faced."

–James Baldwin

Upon the passing of Linda Brown, a former schoolgirl once in the midst of the battle between an all-White Kansas City public school and her being denied access to it, teachers must reflect on how much progress this nation has made since one of the most crucial landmark cases in educational history was decided in 1954 (Romo, 2018). Have U.S. schools permanently removed the barriers to equality in education, or are they still waiting with great anticipation to reach that mountain top? I would argue that schools have not yet arrived. The struggle is *still* real. Yes, they have come a long way, but still have so far to go.

Since the inception of this country, Americans have struggled against themselves to uphold the promises made by the U.S. Constitution and the Declaration of Independence. When Thomas Jefferson declared that "all men are created equal," they struggled with the maintaining of a brutal, yet profitable, centuries-old slave-holding society. As emancipation set enslaved African Americans "free," America continued to struggle to see them as equals. Then, with *Plessy v. Ferguson* (1896), it was declared that "separate" was, in fact, "equal," giving way to Black Codes and Jim Crow Laws for decades to come (Alexander, 2012). However, it was perceived that the struggle of being "separate but equal" was over in 1954, when *Brown v. Board of Education* decided that racially separate public schools were unconstitutional, and measures were put in place to desegregate the nation's educational institutions. Unfortunately, *Brown's* (1954) victory in public education was only on paper because it would take many U.S. schools at least ten years to begin to desegregate after the legislation was passed (Logan & Oakley, 2012).

However, hopes began to lift again in 1960 when the bravery of six-year-old Ruby Bridges and her parents allowed her to be escorted by Federal Marshals into an all-White public school in New Orleans (CBS News, 2002). Even though her innocent presence was met by adults chanting for her removal and death, this pivotal move in the challenge to the resistance of desegregation in the South filled many with the hope that America was still moving in the right direction. Then, in 1964, the country finally reached what looked to be the silver bullet to end the legacy of racism and discrimination, when the Civil Rights Act was passed. Unfortunately, *The Coleman Report*, released in 1965, again shined a bright light on the many mountains still needed to climb in America's pursuit of equal education (Kiviat, 2000). For the next three decades, efforts to desegregate and provide more equitable schooling experiences for marginalized students would continue with *Milliken v. Bradley* (1974), *Board of Education of Oklahoma City Public Schools v. Dowell* (1991), *Missouri v. Jenkins* (1995), and *Sheff v. O'Neill* (1996) (Rivikin, 2016; Eaton, 2007).

Today, however, trends in school zoning suggest that the U.S. has recently entered a state of resegregation, as many students of color attend schools that are overwhelmingly of color and grossly underfunded (Logan & Oakley, 2012). Educational scholar and author Gloria Ladson-Billings (2006) reminds teachers of the "educational debt" owed to millions of poor, immigrant, and other marginalized students when schools seem continuously unable to provide quality education for all students. Educators must be willing to continue to pay back that debt.

The challenges teachers continue to face today are why they must critically examine public schools to make them better for all students. In examining the public school institution, they must look at all of its parts in order to determine which structures and areas are helping in educating all students, and also to be able to consider change and growth in those structures and areas that are not helping in this regard. Schools must evaluate whether teachers are equipped with the proper knowledge and skills; whether curriculums are tainted with bias or founded on truth; and whether relationships are built upon authentic interactions and care. Teachers have to be willing to look at what they thought was "good teaching" and hold it up to the results of academic achievement for proof.

The task set before teachers may pose challenges that many do not want to face. It may be easier for teachers to dismiss the curriculum as racially biased. They may not want to come to terms with how difficult it can be to come to a school that never allows the majority of students to learn anything about themselves. Teachers may look at current disciplinary practices as fair because they have never been subjected to harsher disciplinary actions than another person who also committed the same offense. Teachers may dismiss the prevailing deficit mindsets that lead to lower expectations for students who do not look like them because they have never been judged as inferior or incapable based on how socially connected their parents were, how much money their parents made, or how baggy their jeans were. It may be easy for teachers to dismiss the trauma associated with these practices if they have never experienced such practices themselves. After reading this book, if any teachers are unconvinced that schools are still reeling from the legacy of historical school inequalities, I recommend they watch the docu-series *America to Me* (2018). The students, parents, and teachers at Oak Park and River Forest High School in Chicago are modern-day reminders of that "debt" still owed.

Teachers must not continue to turn a blind eye to these issues because they are not personally affected by them. Please heed this invitation to the acknowledgment of a flawed educational system as I attempt to highlight the current issues in public schools that are not only unfair and unequal but are harming students, in particular, poor students and students of color. Let's not wait until 50 years from now to have to look back on these turbulent times, only to then be able to say yes, there were some issues in the educational system that needed to be solved. Let's turn the tide and be conscious of it now!

As a result of this newly developed consciousness of the problems in our current educational system, I hope to inspire a sense of activism in today's current teaching population to once and for all eradicate the unequal practices in schools and begin focusing on the solutions. Most importantly, I hope to instill a sense of urgency to continue making the necessary changes in this educational system and finally materialize the promises made for an equal educational opportunity for all students.

As current statistics on the standings of schools and students in the United States continue to be appalling, teachers must use these data to inform them of where the most urgent reformation efforts should be focused. According to the National Center for Education Statistics (2015), the U.S. ranks 12th in math, reading, and science, based on results of the Program for International Student Assessment (PISA). These results were compared among other industrialized countries such as Singapore, Japan, and New Zealand. With all of the recent "America First" talk, one has to wonder why America isn't first academically. Nationally, there are a few states that rank better than the entire nation in how they attain more equitable outcomes for their students, but not many. In the United States, North Carolina, Connecticut, and Massachusetts rank as the best in education (Darling-Hammond, 2010). How did they do it? These three states made significant changes in their educational priorities to achieve their success. They all realized that more focus on creating equitable learning experiences for their most marginalized students was an excellent place to start. Unfortunately, many parts of the nation still suffer from disparate racial achievement gaps that signify a continued inability to educate students across racial lines. With African American, Latinx, Native American, and some Asian American students continuously bearing the brunt of this nation's academic underachievement, teachers must admit that there is a problem (Ladson-Billings, 2006). Understanding the unequal educational practices that contribute to the racial achievement gap is essential knowledge for every conscious educator.

The mission of this book is not to deny other factors related to race and students' struggles with gaining access to quality education. I am well aware of what LGBTQ, female, differently abled, migrant, immigrant, bilingual, and English language learning students experience, and the challenges and hurdles they face. Unfortunately, the scope of this book cannot extend into every topic in the manner each topic deserves, as I would need volumes to give everyone the breadth and depth needed to discuss their plight. Even though this book cannot dive into all of the issues all students face, however, many of the approaches and strategies discussed to help close the racial achievement gap can also be applied to help other student populations achieve more equitable outcomes in schools as well.

So, how is it that a country which claims to value the equal educational opportunity for all of its citizens is able to uphold very separate and very unequal school outcomes for the majority of its citizens? The majority of the rest of this book will answer exactly that question. Not only will the remainder of this book provide an introductory, yet foundational understanding of the many issues in current school practices, it will also point teachers in the direction to help remedy those issues in equitable and just ways.

Throughout these next few chapters, I will direct teachers' attention to what I believe to be essential elements in turning around the inequalities experienced in schools and make way for more equitable outcomes to emerge. By examining the benefits of developing a critical consciousness, establishing meaningful and authentic relationships with students, creating a culturally responsive and caring classroom environment, implementing culturally relevant curriculums, and embracing the challenges that come along; teachers will gain a newfound direction in their teaching practices, and finally begin to correct the decades-spanning wrong practices in educating their diverse students.

I hope that by the end of this book more educators will be more conscious of how this nation's public schools have fared in their efforts to provide an equitable education for all of their students. I look forward to more educators becoming more confident in asking how and why public schools continue to suffer from inequitable and discriminatory instructional and disciplinary practices. Once all teachers begin to transform their mindsets about what marginalized students are facing, they will finally begin to see all students as achievers worthy of the efforts needed to make those achievements happen. I hope that teachers can, once and for all, close the achievement gaps prevalent in public schools, and continue to pay back the "educational debt" owed to those affected by it the most (Ladson-Billings, 2006).

In closing, I quote the words of one of the greatest intellectual voices of his time, W.E.B DuBois, words that sufficiently sum up the many promises of education which schools have yet been able to keep:

> *"Of all the civil rights for which the world has struggled and fought for 5,000 years, the right to learn is undoubtedly the*

most fundamental....The freedom to learn....has been bought by bitter sacrifice. And whatever we may think of the curtailment of other civil rights, we should fight to the last ditch to keep open the right to learn, the right to have examined in our schools not only what we believe, but why we believe, what we do not believe; not only what our leaders say, but what the leaders of other groups and nations, and the leaders of other centuries have said. We must insist upon this to give our children the fairness of a start which will equip them with such an array of facts and such an attitude toward truth that they can have a real chance to judge what the world is and what its greater minds have thought it might be."

–W.E.B. DuBois

Ready for the journey? Let's begin.

CHAPTER 1

DEVELOPING A CRITICAL CONSCIOUSNESS

"Shallow understanding from people of goodwill is more frustrating than absolute misunderstanding from people of ill will. Lukewarm acceptance is much more bewildering than outright rejection."

–Dr. Martin Luther King, Jr.
from *Letter from a Birmingham Jail* (1963)

Becoming a conscious educator means not only understanding what students need but also being knowledgeable of the most effective ways to address those needs. However, the journey to becoming a more conscious educator is not an easy one to embark on. It is not a path that all educators will be able to endure, and many may never begin. For those who are willing to challenge the status quo and begin to give all students a fair shot at a quality education, the journey will require some strength and endurance.

The journey towards a more critical consciousness will not be paved with quiet streets and rosy sidewalks. Indeed, this journey will be tough. Those who choose to step out into this wilderness may experience discrimination, mistreatment, being misunderstood, or even excluded from the comforts of being included and welcomed in many school environments (Gorski, 2019). Some may lose friends and make family members uncomfortable, but that is okay. The joy experienced from witnessing the progress of students, improved relationships with parents, and the support from like-minded colleagues will confirm that this road less traveled is worth it.

Developing a critical consciousness is an ongoing learning experience. As teachers continue to live their lives and teach, they will continue to improve their ability to understand and be conscious of the many facets of creating better educational opportunities for all students. Continuing on the path of developing a critical consciousness will continue throughout one's lifetime. Please stay the course. Students will be continuously changing just as the times will continue to progress. Teachers must be dedicated lifelong learners in order to remain effective, and they must be prepared to embrace those changes as they arise. Thankfully, educators do not have to travel this road alone and without guidance. Many scholars and educators have been in the trenches for years, and they offer a few pointers for those just starting today; many of these pointers will be echoed throughout this book.

Self-Reflection is Key

One of the most critical aspects of developing a critical consciousness is self-reflection. Teachers must stop and think about what their beliefs are, where they stem from, and how they affect their teaching practices. Contrary to mainstream lines of thought, teaching is not an objective calling (Slattery, 2013). It is not without bias. Multicultural education scholars Sleeter and Carmona (2017) discuss the importance of teachers identifying their beliefs about teaching and analyzing their effects in the classroom. They remind teachers that deeply embedded in one's beliefs about education lie the roots of why teachers choose to teach, what they teach, and how they teach it. Without self-reflection, educators can and will impose those beliefs onto their students, which can create a disconnect for those students whose cultures, languages, beliefs, and experiences do not mirror those of the educators.

In building a critical consciousness, teachers will be able to bridge those gaps in understanding of their linguistically, ethnically, culturally, and economically diverse students, and create more relevant learning experiences for all. Therefore, teachers must begin to pay close attention to their deeply held beliefs about the world. They must be able to lift the veil of illusion that teachers are unbiased and objective in all they do. In this reflection, we must come to terms with who the majority of teachers are and what they believe.

As of today, 80 percent of America's teaching force racially identifies as White (Miller, 2018). Students, on the other hand, are becoming increasingly more linguistically and ethnically diverse (Pang, 2018). According to Pang (2018, p. 4), there are "50 million K-12 students in the United States from many different racial backgrounds." This means that more than half of the nation's student population is comprised of students of color. These numbers are only expected to increase in the coming years; and, by the year 2025, students of color will make up the majority of the student population (NCES, 2017). In many places they already are. Unfortunately, the growth rates of teachers of color are not increasing at the same rate; in many cases, the number of teachers of color is decreasing (*The Guardian*, 2014). The disparities in teacher demographics versus student demographics may seem like an unimportant factor in determining the quality of education provided for diverse students. Unfortunately, because the majority of teachers in America are White, this fact does create a particular disconnect in the educational success of diverse students, in particular, poor students and students of color. Because White teachers comprise the majority of the teaching force, they are placed in a particular vantage point to help influence more opportunities to enact positive change in public schools. With all that being said, they also have the power to deter it.

To be clear, this is in no way suggesting that White teachers cannot be effective educators for the diverse students in their classrooms. What this chapter will point out is that there are some cultural differences in beliefs, values, and assumptions that can exist between White teachers and their students and parents of color that need to be addressed. It should also be noted that many of the themes throughout this chapter can and do apply to teachers of other ethnic backgrounds as well. Being an African American teacher I, too, have learned many things during my personal journey to becoming a more conscious educator. My middle-class upbringing continues to provide opportunities for growth in areas of class dynamics. However, in recognition of who the majority of the teaching force is, I must explicitly address White teachers. Nonetheless, teachers of other ethnic backgrounds will also benefit from the upcoming discussion. It should be known that being part of a marginalized group does not necessarily equate to an automatic understanding of how inequality and discrimination work in society, nor in public schools. It also does not equate to an automatic commitment to eradicating those inequalities. Many White teachers and teachers of color can be equally invested in maintaining the status quo as long as job opportunities for advancement are at play. No one can be left out of these critical conversations or the opportunity for reflection.

Because of these dynamics, many teachers may avoid discussing topics of race and racism in the classroom. In my experience, particularly in the elementary school setting, there is strong resistance to the mere mention that something racially inappropriate could be at play. Many teachers and administrators may express that any topics surrounding race in the classroom are unacceptable and even inappropriate. To the dismay of many students, issues of inequality are often glossed over in order to maintain the illusion of harmony amongst adults. Maintaining the comfort of White teachers, parents, and students often overrides the needs of those who live with racial inequalities every day. Unfortunately, hang-ups about discussions of race will have to be overcome as educational researchers have uncovered the sad revelation that students (in particularly Black students) as young as preschool-aged can experience not only racial bias from other students but from their teachers as well (Young, 2016). Teachers cannot shy away from these realities due to discomfort. They must instead work through the negative and uncomfortable feelings that can accompany these topics if they are to come out on the other side as more informed and, therefore, more effective educators of ethnically diverse students. Yes, these concepts are difficult to discuss, and, yes, they are intrinsically complex; but the commitment of teachers to their students should be greater than any uncomfortable feelings that may occur in the process. The road to racial equality in schools is rough, and not everyone will make it. But those who do will not only become better educated themselves, they will also be better able to educate their students.

As mentioned above, one of the most critical aspects of developing a critical consciousness is to engage in self-reflection. In the context of becoming a critically conscious teacher, this process involves a more in-depth look into teachers' beliefs about teaching and knowledge about the diverse cultures and perspectives of students. When teachers do not reflect, and are allowed to continue to hold onto their sometimes negative and deficit-oriented assumptions, about their students, their communities, and cultures, they will never get to the heart of the negative racial attitudes that limit the achievement of their diverse students. Without self-reflection in discussing issues of race, teachers may continue to rest in the comfort of what anti-racist educator Robin DiAngelo (2018) calls the "good/bad binary" and never consider the fact that they may have to rethink some deeply held beliefs about race in the classroom.

This "good/bad binary," which is heavily prevalent in the minds of many educators, is the assumption that any unequal, discriminatory, or racist behaviors can only be committed by mean, evil, or immoral people. Because no one would consider themselves evil or immoral, teachers automatically dismiss the importance of addressing any problematic racial insensitivity they may be exhibiting by holding onto the illusion that only bad people can be racist, prejudiced, or discriminatory towards others. Many teachers hold ferociously onto this view and say that they disavow racism; however, many of their actions speak louder than their words. A look at any number of recent news stories highlighting the racist actions of teachers and school leaders tells us that this is true. It was true in Idaho, when teachers proudly dressed up as Mexicans and a "Make America Great Again" wall (Vaglanos, 2018). It was true in Louisiana, when a teacher posted that Black people should stop acting like "animals" (Harris, 2018). It was true in Texas, when a superintendent uttered disparaging remarks about not being able to count on Black quarterbacks (Osborne, 2018). It was also true on a campus at which I worked, where a Hitler-themed movie clip was shown during a faculty meeting to make a joke about the stresses of state testing. When is the Holocaust an appropriate segue into jokes about teachers wearing jeans on testing days? Never, for reflective and conscious educators.

None of those incidents mentioned above were committed with intentional malice or hate. Many of the teachers involved in these incidents were later said to have apologized, and they indicated that they had no ill intent. Unfortunately, when dealing with racism and discrimination, the outcome is what matters most, not the intent. I am sure these teachers truly believed they were doing no harm, but that does not absolve them from consequences, and it does not take away the pain inflicted on their students. When people cause car accidents, they are not absolved from the outcome of their actions simply because they didn't mean to hit someone with their vehicle. The case is the same in instances of teachers exhibiting racist actions and behaviors. They may not have meant to act in such ways. However, they must be held accountable for the actual harm inflicted.

When teachers self-reflect, they can begin to tackle the often contradictory and discriminatory behaviors they may exhibit in contrast to their espoused beliefs of equity and fairness. When teachers are asked to self-reflect, they can begin to examine how disavowing racism is not enough; they must grapple with the aspect of becoming anti-racist (Derman-Sparks & Phillips, 1997). Anti-racist teachers and schools do not rely on their surface proclamations of racial fairness as the extent of their commitment for equity in schools. They do not rely on their willingness to vote for a Black president or political figure. Positive feelings about celebrities and sports athletes are not sufficient either. Anti-racist and therefore conscious educators actively engage in the *disruption* of racism. Critically conscious teachers understand that simple pleas of racial tolerance are not enough to quell the constant negative messages people receive daily about people of color. Critical self-reflection will help teachers examine how the harmful and inaccurate messages received about people of color affect how teachers educate (or fail to educate) their most marginalized students. Understanding how a more in-depth look into teachers' biases and assumptions will help them examine tainted relationships with parents of color due to fear and judgment of the "other." This kind of self-reflection will ultimately help teachers examine how biases taint their relationships with students of color, and cause them to treat those students in less than desirable ways.

DiAngelo breaks down the outcome of the lack of reflection around the "good/bad binary" and the effect it has on educators addressing the presence of possible racist or biased expressions towards their students of color. She concludes:

> *Within this paradigm, to suggest that I am racist is to deliver a deep moral blow — a kind of character assassination. Having received this blow, I must defend my character, and that is where all my energy will go — to deflecting the charge, rather than reflecting on my behavior. In this way, the good/bad binary makes it nearly impossible to talk to white people about racism, what it is, how it shapes all of us and the inevitable ways that*

we are conditioned to participate in it. If we cannot discuss these dynamics or see ourselves within them, we cannot stop participating in racism. The good/bad binary made it effectively impossible for the average white person to understand — much less interpret — racism. (p. 72).

I hope the White teachers who are reading this book are not average. I hope they are as exceptional as I believe them to be, and that is why they are embarking on the journey to becoming more conscious educators. I hope that the many revelations this book presents surrounding issues of race, racism, culture, diversity, equity, and inclusion are met with exceptional responses to action. I hope that the educators on the other side of this book are no longer willing to ignore or deny the racism they see in the world but are, instead, ready to actively engage in eradicating that racism.

To do this, many educators may have to make a shift in their thinking about the inequalities in this country. Taking the hard leap in understanding that America's history is filled with (and founded on) raced-based classifications and inequalities is a history many have tried desperately to hide, minimize, and otherwise avoid (Zinn, 2003; Takaki, 2008; Kendi, 2016). This history, which for many White teachers has been lurking in the shadows, has always been front and center for many people of color. A history that includes when Columbus and his men maimed, slaughtered, and enslaved Indigenous peoples is ever-present as they struggled for sovereignty and land. The history of a Constitution that barred all Blacks, Native Americans, women, and non-land-owning Whites from individual liberties foreshadows the wealth-gaps of today. The Chinese Exclusion Act, the inception of the Jim Crow and Separate but Equal Laws, the mass incarceration of Black and Latinx people, the fight against prejudice towards sexual orientation, and the constant fight for stricter immigration laws currently are daily reminders for many groups in America that they have always lived in a racist and unequal society. Most are just waiting for others to catch up. With these histories in mind, it should be no surprise that schools, which often reinforce the race-based inequalities in society, are not exempt from the necessary reforms to remove them. Therefore, self-reflection amongst educators surrounding personal beliefs and attitudes about diversity, race, and racism is not only key, it is also non-negotiable.

The Basics of Diversity

The effects that these racial disparities have on classrooms, students, and teachers of color are multifaceted, complex, and abundant. The focus of this chapter will not allow the unpacking of every topic, but I will cover what I believe are the most imperative topics. In order to understand the consequences of these effects, teachers have to be conscious of the sources of these disparities and the socially constructed, race-based, and ill-informed ideologies that spawn from them. After that awareness has been made, teachers can then begin to acquire the necessary tools to make sure they are not replicating these inequalities in classrooms despite their best intentions not to. To do so, they must begin their journey in self-reflection by diving into an examination of basic beliefs and ideas about diversity in America. Researchers have identified a few common and prevalent attitudes about diversity that shape America today. The ideas that shape the beliefs behind assimilation, the melting pot, separatism, and cultural pluralism are not only present in America; they are also present within schools today (Koppelman, 2017). Each of these attitudes should be understood and discussed in order to help teachers and schools understand the potentially harmful or problematic outcomes that can occur when negative attitudes about diversity go unchecked amongst educators.

The most traditional idea about diversity comes from the assimilationist. Often assimilationists take on what is called an "all American" attitude towards diversity in America. This attitude often expects all Americans to adopt or assimilate into the dominant, Eurocentric, English-only way of thinking, acting, and believing. Not far behind, the melting pot attitude, although it accepts the diversity that newly immigrated people bring into America, still expects them to mix those ethnic identities into a new American one. On the other hand, the separatist attitude has seen a resurgence through its attempts to segregate diverse peoples. This attitude towards diversity represents a more "us-versus-them" approach reflecting the preference that everyone "stick with their own kind." Finally, in stark contrast is the cultural pluralist attitude. This attitude reflects the idea that all Americans should be able to keep their original cultural and ethnic identities, languages, customs, and beliefs while still adopting, as they see fit, ways of being that also reflect traditional American aspects (Koppelman, 2017). The spectrum of beliefs is wide and ever-evolving.

Teachers need to have a firm understanding of their own ideas and beliefs about diversity when they enter the classroom. As mentioned earlier, classrooms are already more diverse than they were in previous years and are expected to continue to go down that path. In this understanding, teachers need to be able to assess whether the attitudes they hold about how diversity is expressed in America are a hindrance or a help in creating positive and equitable learning environments for their diverse students. To do this, they must analyze how each of these ideas about diversity has played out in either creating more negative or positive experiences for the students subjected to them.

Historically, the idea of assimilation has proved detrimental to the Native and Indigenous persons it was impressed upon. Native American children who were stripped from their families and sent to boarding schools in the nineteenth century to become "Americanized" not only lost their ties to their Native cultural roots; many also lost their entire families because often children who were taken were never returned (Takaki, 2008). The heart-wrenching aftermath of the destructiveness of this practice on Native and Indigenous communities was recently documented in the film, *Dawnland* (2018). Today, assimilationist ideas still play out in schools where the hair of Native and African American students is policed through school dress code policies; in extreme cases, the hair of such students was forcibly removed by teachers in an attempt to conform them to White cultural norms (Wang, 2018; Cherelus, 2018). Sure, enforcing the attitude that everyone acts, thinks, looks, dresses, and speaks the same way may make interacting with culturally and linguistically diverse peoples more convenient for some; but what about the people doing the assimilating? For students who have had to give up, hide, or been punished for being different, the psychological scars inflicted on them have devastating effects on their achievement. Racism and discrimination have all been linked to lower achievement and stress in students who have had to endure it (Anderson, 2016). Assimilating may have felt like the best course of action to help unite all Americans. Unfortunately, as is the case with the melting pot, not everyone is able to be united because their unique differences have kept them as perpetual outsiders.

Melting pot enthusiasts also hope to unite all Americans into one big happy family, with the idea that the mixture of all of the different ethnic and cultural groups in America can all be molded into one brand new American version of themselves. Unfortunately, this idea mimics many of the dominant Eurocentric assumptions of the assimilationist in regards to what an "American" is. For people of color, there has always been one factor that has kept them from truly being valued as an American: Their skin color. Historically and currently, the use of skin color to divide and conquer a nation has worked well for those able to work this practice to their advantage. European immigrants have been the only ones able to be accepted as truly "American." People of color — particularly African, Asian, Native, and Latinx Americans — have had a more difficult time. Many people of color know all too well, that no matter how hard they may try to speak, dress, interact, and communicate as the dominant Eurocentric culture does, they will never be entirely accepted into that culture. Often, those in the dominant group subconsciously understand this and, as a result, often elicit a "color-blind" attitude towards people of color in an attempt to pretend not to notice their differences. Unfortunately, when a person of European descent tells a person of color that they "don't see color, they just see people," it can be taken offensively, as skin color is an essential and proud aspect of many people of colors' identities. At the same time, it is just as equally important to our students. Students of color all around the country feel the effects of a color-blind school system when schools with majorities of minority students are underfunded, when curriculums don't reflect their histories or perspectives, and when teachers regard specific cultural characteristics as deviant or disruptive (Delpit, 2006).

Cultural separatists, on the other hand, have attempted to make diversity matters more cut and dry. Their "us-versus-them" approach was socially acceptable up until 1954, when the Supreme Court ruled in *Brown v. Board of Education* that separate was *not* equal. Although the de jure segregation of the past is no longer legal, there are plenty of instances of de facto segregation that continue to affect the school experiences of poor and students of color in the U.S. today (Rothstein, 2017).

Journalist Nikole Hannah-Jones highlighted the reality many parents of color face in trying to find quality schools for their students when she states: "There's never been a moment in the history of this country where black people who have been isolated from white people have gotten the same resources" (NPR Ed, 2016). These moments, which are heavily dictated by the moving patterns of White parents during episodes of "white flight," leave students of color in schools with fewer resources, fewer qualified teachers, and lower level classes (Gay, 2010). Cultural pluralism, however, seeks to rectify the inequalities experienced by marginalized groups on the receiving end of the three previous perspectives on diversity in our schools, and place a more positive emphasis on their inclusion in American society.

Cultural pluralism rests on the notion that diversity in America is not a problem to be fixed, but an asset to be embraced (Koppelman, 2017). Historically, America has always been a diverse society. Even before the arrival of the first European immigrants, Native and Indigenous peoples could boast of the diversity that resided between tribes in their languages, customs, and beliefs. After the arrival of European immigrants, which also ushered in the beginnings of enslavement for Africans, followed the migrations of the Chinese, Japanese, Irish, Jewish, and Filipino peoples as well. These migrations, which were the result of a perceived increase in economic opportunity, also brought about more changes (and challenges) to the diversity of America. This nation's long-standing disputes between territories with Mexico have also increased the nation's exposure to many different customs, values, languages, and beliefs since its founding (Takaki, 2008; Zinn, 2006; Koppelman, 2017). Unfortunately, reactions to this diversity have not always reflected espoused beliefs of liberty, equality, freedom, and justice for all. Cultural pluralism seeks to change that.

Reflected in the ideas of cultural pluralism is the notion that all people should be valued and accepted for who they are. Cultural pluralism doesn't seek to simply tolerate differences, but to embrace and understand those differences in order to build better relationships between groups. Pluralism doesn't require anyone to deny their cultural origins and replace them with one more reflective of the dominant group. It says there is not just one way of thinking, acting, knowing, or living. It accepts the differences that diverse groups bring to the table, and says that individuals can be who they are *and* be Americans at the same time. Historically, schools have had a hard time moving towards a more pluralist approach to teaching and learning, and have often maintained assimilationist practices in their expectations for students (Gay, 2010; Howard, 2016). Schools have often promoted the importance of individuality; yet, they often maintain strict adherence to conformity amongst their students. This adherence is reflected in expectations for styles of dress, hair, communication, interaction styles, perspectives, curriculums, and the like. This strict adherence to Eurocentric ways of thinking, acting, and being has had devastating effects on diverse students in schools.

However, schools that have managed to break the chains of conformity and allowed themselves to embrace the benefits of a truly culturally diverse learning environment can serve as role models for those still struggling. With examples like the Algebra Project, the Lemon Grove Project, and many other school models, teachers can begin to see that when the unique identities, talents, histories, and experiences of students are brought into the classroom, learning not only becomes more meaningful, it becomes more relevant and engaging, too (Pang, 2018). Teachers must be able to reflect and understand how views on diversity impact the experiences they provide or do not provide for their diverse students. In these reflections, if teachers conclude that they may not have the most positive attitudes towards diversity, then they must be willing to make the necessary adjustments that can lead to more positive and productive outcomes. Teachers must be willing to challenge their deeply held beliefs and increase their knowledge around issues and events surrounding race and culture in schools.

The Basics of Race

In continuing to increase critical consciousness, educators must not only address their attitudes about diversity, but they must also understand the basics of what culture, race, and racism are to be able to dismantle any negative attitudes that perpetuate it properly. With that in mind, it must first be acknowledged that race in and of itself does not exist (Sussman, 2014; Pang, 2018; T.C. Howard, 2010). Gasp! Everyone is human, and there are no inferior or superior races as some pseudoscientists (and politicians) would have people continue to believe (Pang, 2018). Race, however, is a social construct invented centuries ago to justify the enslavement and ill-treatment of Native, African, Latinx, Asian and (some) European peoples throughout the height of the European slave-trade (Kendi, 2016; Takaki, 2008).

Unfortunately, these justifications for the ill treatment of those whose land was taken, and whose kidnapping and forced labor was used to build this nation, still exist today, even 150 years after slavery was abolished (Kendi, 2016). Even though race has no biological significance, teachers still must be efficient in their understanding of how "race" works in a racialized society in order to understand how it affects diverse students in schools.

The European slaveholding elites that contrived racial myths about the inferiority of diverse people were so convincing in their explanations for the differences found in groups of people around the globe that throughout history those same justifications have been used to wipe out and commit cultural genocide on any group deemed less than worthy of life (Zinn, 2003). Whether teachers like it or not, race and racist ideas are ingrained in this country's culture and makeup. White people and people of color have all been breathing in the "smog" of racist ideas since the first slave ship landed in Jamestown in 1619 (Tatum, 1997). One can even look further than that with the accidental inquisitions of Christopher Columbus in 1492 in his dealings with the Taino and Arawak peoples he encountered in the Caribbean (Bigelow & Peterson, 1998). Throughout American history, people of color have always been deemed as savage, barbaric, backward, uncivilized, less than, or not human and therefore not worthy to be treated with equal human value to those deemed (in the eyes of Europeans) "civilized" (Takaki, 2008). Today, these same race-based justifications for the mistreatment and disregard of people of color can be seen in the mass incarceration rates of African American and Latinx peoples, in the disproportionate rates of police brutality in communities of color, and the overall disparaging statistics that highlight the lack of access to quality health care, education, employment, and wealth gaps for people of color (Martinovitch, 2017; Alexander, 2012). Race is an unfortunate part of many peoples' everyday experiences and perceptions of themselves and others. It affects standards of beauty, perceptions of intelligence, and even who people deem as desirable for a mate and procreation. Ignoring the far-reaching effects racism has had on society and students would be an egregious act of willful ignorance.

Even with all this evidence, many teachers may still be unconvinced that issues of race have relevance within schools. After all, various legislations have been passed, and citizens are no longer separate; people have civil rights, and the pendulum continues to swing towards justice every day. This is all true. However, the long history of race and racism, although outlawed on the books, still remains deep in the hearts of many. These deeply held beliefs about the superiority and inferiority of different groups in America continue to play out in public policies and in peoples' interactions with others. They also play out in teacher interactions with students. Educators must become knowledgeable about these dynamics.

In a race-based society such as the U.S., membership in certain racial groups gives certain people advantages and creates a disadvantage for others. Whites have historically had a systematic advantage. On the contrary, those "others" placed in subordinate roles (people of color) are "systematically disadvantaged" (Tatum, 1997). Still, some educators may be thinking that none of this applies to them, that they do not consider themselves to be in a position of advantage and they certainly do not think of themselves as "better" than anyone else. Please do not take this analysis as personal attacks on White teachers or White people in general. Those teachers may be very sincere in their pleas at fairness. To develop the critical consciousness necessary to eradicate these inequalities, teachers need to understand how the race-based *system* works in this country. They have to understand that these discussions are not merely about White people, but *white supremacy*. It is not just about what individuals do or don't do; it is also about how one's position in this society can have significant effects on their access to opportunities or the lack of access to opportunity experienced by others. In her pivotal book, *Why Are All The Black Kids Sitting Together in the Cafeteria*, Beverly Daniel Tatum (1997) further examines how the roles of dominant and subordinate group membership work:

> *Dominant groups, by definition, set the parameters within which the subordinates operate. The dominant group holds power and authority in society relative to the subordinates and determines how that power and authority may be acceptably used. Whether it is reflected in determining who gets the best jobs, whose history will be taught in school, or whose relationships will be validated by society, the dominant group has the most significant influence in determining the structure of the society* (Tatum, 1997, p.23).

This fact is the reason why White people are the majority in leading positions in business, medicine, government, and education (DiAngelo, 2018). How can teachers know if the dominant/subordinate roles society has placed on people also exist within the walls of public schools? Teachers know it exists when students are chastised for not using "proper" English. It can be seen when teachers disregard the literary, scientific, and mathematical contributions of people of color and do not include them on their displays of "great" scientists, mathematicians, and authors. Instead, they only display their achievers of color posters on special occasions, during festivals, or in a special unit. When educators are unable to see or value the cultural differences among their students, it can cause them to devalue the home life of poor students and students of color. They may devalue the sense of community, resilience, and faith that their parents and extended family members may have used to help teach them up until their arrival in classrooms. Instead, they may only view the low-income and culturally different backgrounds of their students in terms of what they "don't have" in comparison to "whiteness" instead of seeing all the knowledgeable cultural assets that they come to school with.

When teachers cannot see the value of the cultures their diverse students come to school with, they may miss the poetic nature, analogical reasoning, and complexity in Black English when their African American students speak (Gay, 2010). They may miss the importance of including the mathematical, scientific, and literary advancements and contributions of ancient African and Mayan societies so that all students can see positive representations of themselves and others. They may miss the sense of responsibility and communalism inherent in many students who rush home every day to go to work, take care of siblings, or help ailing grandparents or relatives. There are so many valuable assets diverse students come to school with that may lie outside of the Eurocentric norms many have come accustomed to. When one cannot see the value of anything outside of those norms, vast amounts of talent, intellect, and potential already within diverse students never get the acknowledgment they deserve. Teachers especially see the effects of these dominant social paradigms when the majority of the teaching force is White. Schools can no longer deny its existence.

When the majority of the teaching population is from the dominant group and the majority of the student population is not, there is an uneven power structure at play. When teachers are unaware of how this power plays out in their classrooms, it can have devastating effects on the achievement of students of color. In Gary R. Howard's (2016) unapologetic *We Can't Teach What We Don't Know*, he writes of his journey in becoming a conscious educator and the obstacles many White educators face in doing the same. In his book, he highlights the lack of exposure many White people have in interacting with anyone different from themselves. He cites research from the Public Religion Research Institute that revealed: "over 90% of White American's social interactions are with other White people, less than 10% with people of color" (Howard, 2016, p.18). This social isolation of White people from people of color results in what Howard (2016) calls a "luxury of ignorance." This "luxury" is what keeps many White Americans from understanding how race and racism affect the people of color who do not have the privilege to escape it. This ignorance of other people's struggle for racial equality in America is also what keeps America's long-held myth of meritocracy alive and well. The idea that those that work hard and are smart will be successful or prosperous, whereas those that are not must be lazy or unintelligent is a powerful and prevalent belief among many Americans; especially teachers. This belief left unchallenged misses the reality of many people of color in which structural or institutional racism often determines how successful one may become.

This "luxury" in being able to be ignorant of the plight of others leads many teachers to internalize the false notion that any group still suffering from the ills of the past must be making a choice to do so, and therefore are not worthy of empathy, understanding, and action still needed to maximize their learning experience in the classroom. In this instance, ignorance is not bliss; in fact, it has unseen consequences for those who have the privilege to live in it and devastating ones for those whose humanness is defined by it. Thus, in order for teachers to be more effective for their diverse students, they must grow their knowledge and understanding of many of the complex realities people of color find themselves in by opening themselves up to discussions about significant issues in educational racial and cultural matters — racism, bias, and privilege.

What is Racism?

Let's begin by clearing up a few common misconceptions about racism. First, it is not racist to discuss issues of racism. Second, it is also not racist to point out instances of racism. These common responses to discourses focused on race are just attempts to shut the conversation down and are a reflection of the lack of "racial stamina" the accuser is suffering from (DiAngelo, 2018). It comes as no surprise that these topics can bring out feelings of discomfort in many people. We are a nation built on the idea of racism, yet to expose that reality has been deemed the ultimate taboo in many circles. Finally, White people *cannot* experience racism. As long as White people remain the dominant racial group in America, they *cannot* experience racism. Prejudice, yes. Bias, yes. Rudeness, absolutely. But racism, no. Reverse racism is not a thing as well. This is not a two-way street. It is crucial that all educators interested in eradicating racist and discriminatory practices in their schools understand these critical points. Teachers must all have a shared understanding of these issues before any positive changes can be made.

In actuality, racism is defined by anti-racist educators and authors Louise Derman-Sparks and Carol Brunson Phillips (1997) as "an institutionalized system of economic, political, social, and cultural relations that ensures that one racial group has and maintains power and privilege over all others in all aspects of life" (p.2). They continue by elaborating on the importance of the outcomes of racism in stating that "the outcome of the individual, cultural, and institutional policies and actions, rather than the intent behind them, determines the presence of racism" (p.9). Again, because of the racialized nature of America, White people have been afforded more institutional power. This is why no one but White people can be racist in America. Because of this power, when White people hold racist or negative views about people of color, their jobs become jeopardized, their access to healthcare becomes fragile, and in the case of schools, marginalized students suffer underachievement and failure. Racism is not just about individuals with mal intentions; racism works best when that racial prejudice is met with institutional power (Derman-Sparks & Brunson Phillips, 1997). That was the ultimate goal in its design. This lack of understanding leads many educators to be under the impression that if they do not mean to be "racist," then their actions should never be identified as such. This is not the case. For many people of color, the outcomes of racist actions (intended or not) which result in discrimination, the devaluing of one's personhood, or death cannot be excused because the offending party did not mean it. All actions have consequences. The best way for teachers to reduce the risk of participating in or perpetuating racism is to understand what it is and what it is not. Because all Americans have been breathing in the toxic fumes of racist ideas since the inception of this country, it is possible not to intend to be racist and still hold racist beliefs and exhibit racist actions. Educators must be aware of how both manifest themselves.

In the context of schools, the institution of racism has taken on many forms. Historically, it came in the form of denying access to enslaved Africans and their children to any form of education during slavery. Any of the enslaved caught learning or knowing how to read, could be subject to severe beatings, dismemberment, or even death. After abolition, institutional racism continued in the form of segregated schooling for many groups of color, including African, Chinese, Jewish, Latinx, and Native American children (Pang, 2018). In some of the most extreme cases of racism in schools, as mentioned before, Native American children endured decades of being forcefully removed from their homes and placed in Indian boarding schools throughout the U.S. and Canada to forcefully assimilate Native American children to White cultural norms (Bear, 2008).

Today, racism in public schools has been able to go unseen and under the radar for many as current educational practices and policies have taken on more race-neutral terms. Today's public schools no longer overtly segregate students; they provide "school choice." They no longer bus low-income students of color into more wealthy and White schools; they just shut down any low performing schools that fail to meet state standards. The government no longer restricts access to education; it just provides lower quality teachers, facilities, and resources for low-income and students of color (Darling-Hammond, 2010). Ample research shows that the amount of money given to majority White schools equals well over $23 billion more than what is provided for schools with majority populations of color (Folley, 2019). Today, although racism may be invisible to some, racism in schools still reeks from the stench of lack of quality teachers, curriculum, and the school-to-prison pipeline (Prager, 2011; Resmovlts, 2014). Today many students of color go to schools with teachers that are not certified and have fewer years of experience than their White and wealthier counterparts whose schools are not only stocked with more experienced teachers but higher paid ones as well (Resmovlts, 2014). Students of color, particularly Black, are also disciplined more harshly and more often, and have been arrested or removed by police three times the rate of their White counterparts who commit similar offenses (Resmovlts, 2014).

Currently, the presence of these disparities is at the heart of recent debates over arming teachers in schools. As contested as this topic is, any discussion without the recognition of these disparities should be dismissed for lack of context over concerns. When teachers, mainly White, are unaware of how racism plays out in schools, they can knowingly or unknowingly perpetuate racism within their classrooms and maintain the current status quo of underachievement for many of our marginalized groups of students. In the case of guns for teachers, they could harm their students even if they do not intend to do so. The unconscious bias many teachers hold about people different from themselves cannot be underestimated as it is the root cause for many of these disparaging circumstances.

What is Bias?

As mentioned above, racism is not a two-way street. Bias, however, is not an institutionalized system of power and privilege. Bias is a human condition. Everyone has a bias. Bias is the belief system that people operate from. In the context of understanding race in our schools, racial bias is "a conscious or unconscious prejudice against an individual or group based on their identity" (Collins, 2018). Implicit or unconscious racial bias is what leads to the perpetuation of racism in many public schools. Because of this, teachers have to check their bias.

Implicit bias has had a recent surge of attention in the news with instances of White people calling the police on Black people for particularly benign reasons. From barbequing in an Oakland park, to selling water on a hot day, to moving into one's apartment, implicit racial bias seems to have run rampant in the lives of everyday Americans. Unfortunately, racial bias is not a new phenomenon. In the words of famous actor Will Smith, "racism is not getting worse; it's just getting filmed." Unfortunately, I know this too well, from my own experiences with people calling the police on me because they did not like the breed of dog I owned, or because I would not go and "fetch" a dog toy from that dog. If I had thought to video my unfortunate incidents, there would have been a few #DogParkDanas going viral on many Facebook feeds. I know the irrational outcomes associated with bias all too well.

Bias is a tricky concept for many people to grasp, as noted earlier because most are only keen on identifying the overt, David Duke brand of bias and racism. Bias, because it can manifest itself in conscious or unconscious beliefs, many do not know it is there. However, one's actions can provide proof of its existence. Because of the many negative messages received about diverse people, from television, movies, and mass media, bias comes to light in many different ways. Racial bias can be observed when someone crosses the street to avoid walking next to a group of young Black males. It can be seen when a police officer shoots an unarmed person of color because they "feared" for their lives. It can be seen when a person calls for police intervention in the reporting of the everyday activities of law-abiding people of color. These biases lead many to consciously or unconsciously maintain the centuries-old practice and belief that people of color need to be controlled, are threatening, more dangerous, and overall inferior to others.

Implicit racial bias can also be seen in schools and is most evident when looking at the disparaging discipline rates between African, Latinx, and Native American students and their White counterparts (NECS, 2017). Unfortunately, there are numerous studies and research that reveal that when teachers carry unchecked implicit bias about their poor and students of color, they lower their expectations, discipline them more harshly, and refer them for special education services at higher rates than their White counterparts (Safir, 2016). In 2018 alone, teachers and administrators made headlines when they posted and tweeted racist remarks, and even dressed up and took pictures in racist and stereotypical costumes (Osborne, 2018; Harris, 2018; Vaglanos, 2018). Every one of the educators involved in these incidents claimed to value their students of color and had no ill intent behind the racist and bias actions they perpetuated. As noted earlier, good intentions are not enough. Teachers must be able to show it through their actions. Thankfully, there are many ways in which teachers can actively reduce the effects of their racial bias on the diverse students in their care. The Kirwan Institute for Race and Ethnicity (2014) has done extensive research on measures to reduce the effects of implicit bias in the classroom. These measures include:

- Providing supports for struggling students.

- Revising discipline policies to make sure they are fair.

- Providing teachers with cultural competency training which focuses on the reduction of "cultural deficit" thinking, and the understanding of racial bias.

- Promoting authentic and positive relationships between teachers and their diverse students.

- Implementing Positive Behavioral Interventions and Supports (PBIS).

Still, recognizing racial biases can be a challenging and difficult experience. Many teachers may avoid this crucial process and rely on their proximity to people of color for the "proof" that these types of biases do not apply to them. I have seen this in action many times and have been used as the token to deflect such claims. Unfortunately, it does not matter how many spouses, dates, children, grandchildren, in-laws, relatives, friends, or co-workers of color one may have. All are susceptible to unconscious racial biases simply because all have been exposed to the constant and persistent negative stereotyping of people different from themselves. Only through the hard work of tackling these biases can teachers begin to reduce their effects on the students in their care. Avoidance of these topics by teachers is resulting in life-altering repercussions for many students. The discomfort one may experience in coming to terms with many of the realizations mentioned above is critical, not just for teachers, but for our students. Teachers invested in overturning inequality can no longer afford to live within the privileges of not knowing.

What is Privilege?

Yes, privilege must be discussed: White privilege to be exact. Not only does it have to be discussed, but it must be understood how this polarizing term operates and the implications of it in classrooms and schools. Peggy McIntosh (1989), in her classic paper *White Privilege: Unpacking the Invisible Knapsack*, exposes White privilege, what it looks like, and what tools can help dismantle and end it. In a nutshell, McIntosh explains White privilege as "unearned advantage and conferred dominance" (McIntosh, 1989). She begins by exposing the prevalent (albeit false) narrative of what racism is. She states, "I was taught to recognize racism only in individual acts of meanness by members of my group, never in invisible systems conferring unsought racial dominance on my group from birth." She continues that the "obliviousness" of White privilege is kept intact "so as to maintain the myth of meritocracy, the myth that democratic choice is equally available to all" (McIntosh, 1989). She continues to describe it as unearned privilege that simply breaks down into assets given to White Americans in which they can count on to "cash in" at their convenience" (McIntosh, 1989). I have witnessed the "cashing in" of these assets within the walls of schools.

In order to understand how White privilege has continued to operate so seemingly unnoticed in schools and in the minds of many teachers, one must first break down what these privileges and the conferred dominance McIntosh implies looks like in schools. Typically, these assets come in the form of the dominant cultural norms expected and reinforced throughout school culture. Because those in the dominant group hold the majority of teaching and administrative positions, many school expectations for communicating, interacting, dressing, and believing stem from White cultural norms. Many students already familiar with the dominant ways of thinking, acting, and interacting may find it easier to experience success because they are already familiar with the dominant cultural expectations of teachers and administrators. Students who may come from cultural backgrounds that think, act, and believe in ways outside of those norms may be viewed as different, disruptive, unintelligent, and even a disciplinary concern simply because they do not carry themselves in ways that are "acceptable" within White cultural norms. As a result, many of these students are subject to lower teacher expectations, harsher discipline practices, and placed in low-level or remedial track classes due to these cultural differences (Banks, 2019; Gay, 2010; Howard, 2010). The maintenance of dominant cultural norms is prevalent and observable throughout many everyday school practices.

In public schools, these privileges can be seen in the curriculum that is taught in which much of the history, literature, communication, and writing styles reflect that of White cultural norms. It can be seen in dress code policies in which students of color and many of their culturally relevant hairstyles such as locks, braids, or dreads are deemed inappropriate for the school setting. Native American students, particularly boys, are often admonished for their culturally relevant style of long hair. An example of how far some teachers will go in maintaining these dominant cultural norms amongst students was demonstrated when a teacher was so offended by her Native American student's wearing of his long hair, that she took it upon herself to not only call him a slur but to cut it (McKee, 2018).

More subtle and less overt instances occur when holidays such as Thanksgiving or Christmas take center stage, leaving other holidays to remain in the margins of lessons or in a separate unit (if there is time). Often, even when diverse holidays are introduced, they are frequently viewed through an explicit Eurocentric lens, often minimizing sacred cultural beliefs to fun festivals and costume parties. The aesthetic makeup of schools also plays a role in maintaining these norms as students walk down hallways covered with posters of famous artists, scientists, mathematicians, and historical figures that almost exclusively hail from European origins. As a primary teacher, I was always dismayed in the lack of understanding of representation. Too many students of color are forced to represent themselves in self-portraits with paper and crayons that look nothing like them, all in the name of uniformity and cuteness.

In matters of school discipline, it is observed in the over-policing of students of color in social settings, or the given benefit-of-the-doubt to non-black students in situations instead of being instantly viewed with suspicion. However, the ultimate privilege is in being seen as the "norm" and the barometer in which all other groups of people are held up to. This barometer often determines one's worthiness of respect, dignity, love, and forgiveness.

Consequently, to fully understand White privilege and other insidious forms of racial bias, we cannot oversimplify its existence in terms of good or bad. I caution teachers in assuming that having privilege means the one who holds it has done so purposefully and should be ashamed or feel guilty. It should also never be concluded that one who holds any privilege has had a life free from disappointment, trauma, or hard work. Holding privilege only means that, because of it, there may be some things one does not experience. In the same way, just because some lack certain privileges does not mean their lives have been damned to misfortune and ruin. It only means that there may be some opportunities not afforded to them that cannot be overcome by hard work and the pulling up of one's "bootstraps." Teachers have to understand that these issues are complex and can be confusing especially when one can turn on the television or radio and listen to multi-millionaire people of color living out their dreams. That's great for them, yet it doesn't erase the realities of many people of color and their lack of access to these opportunities. Even for these high-paid athletes, entertainers, and professionals, racism never goes away. One doesn't just price out of oppression. It's crucial to understand the dynamics of privilege and disadvantage do not affect everyone in the same way to the same degree, and any exception to these rules will never negate the rule.

Intersectionality

These roles of dominant and subordinate, privilege and disadvantaged, have intersectional implications that many flow in and out of as well. One can hold any of these positions at some point, depending on the value that society places on their identities. Researchers have identified the desirable groups in American society and often refer to them as "ups" (Koppelman, 2017). People often categorized as such tend to identify as White, male, heterosexual, English-speaking, non-disabled, middle or upper class, and Christian. On the other hand, the "downs" can typically identify as a person of color, female, non-Christian, non-English speaker, disabled, lower class, or a member of the LGBTQ community. However, who is seen as an "up" or a "down" highly depends on the context and situation each individual is in. For example, as a light-skinned African American, I may hold an advantage over a darker-skinned African American. As heterosexual, I may hold an advantage over a gay or lesbian identifying person. As middle-class, I may hold an advantage over a lower-income individual. As college educated, I may hold an advantage over a non-degreed person. As a Christian, I may hold an advantage over someone who practices Islam, Judaism, Hinduism, Sikhism, or no faith at all. I, too, hold certain privileges over someone else who may not "fit" into those advantaged categories in American society. Again, it is essential to note that these advantages and disadvantages may not be felt to the same degree or experienced in the same way as another person, but that does not mean its presence cannot be acknowledged. Again, having a privileged identity does not mean one's life has been rainbows and butterflies, just as having a disadvantaged identity does not render one to a life of misfortune.

If educators truly believe that "all men are created equal," they need to do the hard work of examining themselves and their privileges to see what can be done to help overturn the oppression in communities and schools. Whether families or persons are responsible for the injustices of the past or not, many are reaping the benefits of a racist and discriminatory past as others still bear the scars of its consequences. As educators "fettering out the systemic nature of institutional racism as educational practice, and holding it up to the light, should be a noble and necessary function of the educator" (Givens, 2007, p. 163). However, teachers have to be committed to doing this together. No one teacher, administrator, school, or district can do it alone. All teachers need to be willing to work toward becoming a more conscious educator so that they can all create a more significant impact in helping overturn the unequal practices running rampant in schools.

If 80 percent of the teaching force is comprised of White, middle-class Americans, who have had little to no social interaction with people of color throughout their lives, how can they effectively educate children from diverse backgrounds? It can only be done effectively if one is committed to be exposed to the authentic knowledge of other cultures, histories, and struggles; otherwise, the myths of cultural inferiority will continue to be enforced. Relying on good intentions, half-truths, and distortions of the nation's history in its business of oppression have kept not only citizens and teachers from being the proprietors of truth and knowledge, but it has also made many accomplices in maintaining the oppressive systems established centuries ago. In this journey of becoming a more conscious educator, teachers must continue to look at many of the deeply held beliefs and views that many educators hold onto, that prohibit the growth needed to reach all students without bias. To move on from the practices of a racist educational past, show a true value for all students, and care about their individual needs, teachers must continue to examine their deeply held beliefs about race, racism, diversity, and culture in schools. Next, an examination of the practice of one of the most detrimental yet widespread cultural ideologies that have prevented many from moving towards a more culturally aware perspective: color blindness.

CHAPTER 2

TO SEE OR NOT TO SEE

"The core of 'I don't see color,' is 'I don't see my own color, I don't see difference because my race and culture is the center of the universe.'"

–Randy Ross, Brown University

O nce during a neighborhood get together, I became engaged with one of my neighbors in a conversation about the ideology of color blindness. This conversation did not start as a formal introduction to the topic of race relations. Like many neighborly conversations, it stemmed from chit chat about the happenings in our daily lives. During this particular conversation, my neighbor was discussing with me the recent transition her children had made from a majority White, private, Christian school to the public and very diverse high school in the neighborhood. During this exchange, a few things stuck out to me. After noting her fears for her children in attending the new high school with "those kids," she quickly went into a story about how proud she was of her daughter for bringing home diverse groups of friends and never mentioning their race to her mother. This seemed like a proud moment for my neighbor to be able to say that her daughter "didn't see color" when she selected her friends. I could tell that she was very pleased with the direction the conversation was going; however, I had to interrupt her story, "What is wrong with being able to see color?"

What is Color Blindness?

Color blindness is "a response to race based on the belief that a person should not notice or consider the skin color of another" (Koppelman, 2017). When teachers or administrators claim they are "color-blind" and therefore do not see "race" and "treat everyone the same," this is a clear indication that there is a lack of understanding of the importance of race and the role it plays in a student's identity. It is also an indication of the need to understand how to create more equitable, meaningful, and relevant learning opportunities for all students. Contrary to popular ideological narratives, Americans do not live in a "color-blind" post-racial society. Furthermore, racism and discrimination will not just go away if people stop talking about it or pretend it doesn't exist. It doesn't work that way. Unfortunately, due to the legacy and lingering effects of oppression and discrimination of marginalized groups, society is still wrought with many racial, ethnic, gender, sexual identity, and class inequalities and conflicts (Martinovitch, 2017). Although, I understand the desire of clinging to the thought that one should be "color-blind" as a sign or symbol of one's ability to be fair and equal, living in this state of racial blindness only symbolizes one's inability to acknowledge the very different and often unequal experiences of others (T.C. Howard, 2010). Because of living in a racialized society that heavily places value and often devalues people based off of their racial identities, teachers who lack the cultural knowledge in understanding how this reality can affect the academic achievement of their diverse students are often not very effective for them.

In the context of teaching culturally and linguistically diverse students, if teachers cannot "see" their students, it makes it that much more challenging to teach them. When teachers choose to ignore the racial and ethnic differences in the experiences, histories, and perspectives of their diverse students, it becomes that much more difficult to make learning experiences relevant, meaningful, and equitable for them (Scruggs, 2009). Teachers who cannot see the individual differences in students based on their racial identities can often misinterpret what could be a simple cultural difference and turn it into aggression, a lack of respect, or a lack of ability. In actuality, this ideology of color blindness is one of those "good intentions" that are deceptively harmful in practice. This myth, if left unchallenged in the mindset of educators, will continue to be the catalyst in the perpetuation of unequal practices in educational settings. This myth, however, is not quickly abolished. This myth has been so pervasive and widespread due to its association with the often-whitewashed legacy of Dr. Martin Luther King, Jr.; it has left a permanent stain in the racial psyche of many Americans (Koppelman, 2017). The common reference to Dr. King as the purveyor of "color blindness" has not only grossly misinterpreted and perverted his legacy, but has served to perpetuate and preserve the racism he, and others like him, valiantly disavowed (Benbow, 2018).

The Myth of Color Blindness

Those who grew up during the time when Dr. Martin Luther King, Jr. was alive may remember that the Civil Rights leader that is now hoisted up every January in professing America's commitment towards racial equality was not always viewed as a treasured "national hero" (Benbow, 2018). Many White citizens and politicians had very harsh and vile views about this iconic hero and the messages he promoted. At one point, he was so hated that J. Edgar Hoover himself called him "the most notorious liar in the country" (Gage, 2014). Our government so hated Dr. King to the extent that the FBI sent him a letter telling him to kill himself (Gage, 2014). If one recalls, he is no longer on this earth, and it's not because he passed from old age. One may be wondering, *What could Dr. King have done to deserve such treatment?* Historical amnesia is a common phenomenon and can be easily remedied with a little something called historical truth and analysis.

A close look at any number of his speeches (in their entirety) and writings such as *Letter from a Birmingham Jail* (1963) will give people a clear sense of Dr. King's goals. It was not a color-blind society that ignored the racial differences of others; it was quite the opposite. When he uttered those famous words in his most famous *Dream* (1963) speech, he was not calling for people not to see one's blackness, but instead to *recognize* it and *affirm* it as just as valuable as whiteness. He was calling for the recognition of African American contributions in helping build the U.S. into what it is today. He was calling for the recognition of African American history as relevant and as worthy of study as European history. He was calling for the recognition that even though African Americans suffered greatly during slavery, slavery in America was not the total of African American history. He was calling for the affirmation of African American culture to be seen as valid and noble as it had to be recreated during enslavement when their native African roots were beaten out of them and forbidden. Unfortunately, this kind of affirmation of blackness has generationally been challenging (and upsetting) to many White people. It is as if in recognizing the validity of being an African American as human and worthy of all the "equal protection" as Whites that somehow Whites will lose out? This is just not true. In the famous words of Civil Rights activist Cesar Chavez when discussing the merits of respecting other cultures, he says that in doing so does not "require contempt or disrespect for other cultures." Black, Indigenous, and other peoples of color loving themselves does not equal automatic hate towards whites. It just doesn't equate.

Using Dr. King's legacy as an excuse to ignore or deny how race and racism still affects people today helps no one in their pursuit of racial equality. In reality, the twisting of Dr. King's words and the false sense of the finality of racism after the Civil Rights Act (1965) was passed, only ensured one thing: that the blatant and vile racist beliefs still lingering in the hearts of many would no longer be socially acceptable. Now, overt racism is out and the new covert racism is in. This "new racism" doesn't beat people of color over the head with rocks and billy clubs, or hang them from ropes in trees. This new racism smiles, uses race-neutral language in creating discriminatory public policies, and tries to maintain that racism no longer exists because one cannot "see" it.

The Pitfalls of Color Blindness

When teachers possess color blind views about the diverse students in their classrooms, they can inadvertently reinforce the dominant notion that their students are "just like me" and miss the important variations that racial, ethnic, and cultural differences play in students' language, beliefs, perspectives, experiences, and interaction styles. By being unaware of the cultural differences among their students, teachers can inadvertently force their cultural ways of thinking, acting, and knowing onto their diverse students and create a cultural conflict in the classroom. These cultural conflicts often place students who behave outside of the dominant cultural norms of the teacher or the school to be subject to lower teacher expectations because the educator has misinterpreted simple cultural differences and relegated them to misbehaviors or deviant behavior (Scruggs, 2009).

These lowered expectations often affect poor, students of color, English language learners, and students with disabilities the most (Koppelman, 2017). Ample research has shown that these lowered expectations of marginalized students are a significant contributor to the current racial disparities in academic achievement observed today (Gay, 2010; Valencia, 2010; Howard, 2016). These lowered expectations allow teachers to rely on cultural deficit thinking, which often devalues the homes and cultures of their poor and students of color (Valencia, 2010). These lowered expectations manifest themselves when teachers assign remedial content to seemingly unmotivated students and settle it in their minds that "these kids can't handle" more challenging work (Books, 2007). It manifests itself when teachers reduce the intellect of students of color by the way they look, dress, and speak. It also allows teachers to be then surprised by the achievement of students of color and then, on occasion, proceed to accuse them of cheating (Wang, 2019). This is not just the case for low-income urban schools. I witnessed the widespread effects of lowered expectations when I saw that the disparities in the achievement rates of African American students at my affluent suburban campus were just as apparent as the low-income campus I previously worked at. Yes, research has shown that even when income is accounted for, even suburban students of color perform at lower rates than their White counterparts (Logan & Oakley, 2012). Not only does color blindness lead teachers not to see the abilities of their diverse students, it can also lead them to disregard the importance of their history and identity as well.

When schools are not conscious of the misguided intentions of color blindness, they will ignore the importance of affirming the racial identities of their students. They will ignore the need for students of color to see positive images of themselves reflected to them in their everyday curriculum. As a result, their histories, perspectives, and values will be reduced to side notes only to be seen on special occasions, if at all. Two poignant experiences during my teaching career illustrate the far-reaching effects of color blindness on the learning experiences of students and the working environments of teachers of color alike.

The concepts of diversity and inclusion and what it should look like in a school setting are interpreted and expressed in various ways across the nation. I have not experienced many schools whose approach to diversity could not be summed up by a once a year festival-type activity or the special reading of celebratory history facts during the morning announcements. A school campus where I once taught was no exception, and their understanding of diversity played out during their annual multicultural festival as well. At this particular campus, I was newly hired when they announced the upcoming festival. I was unfamiliar with the planning process for the "International Festival," and I was curious to see how it would be conducted. I was interested to see how a school with such a growing diversity of teachers and students would celebrate all the various cultural backgrounds that attended the school. To my dismay, this campus was not very diverse or inclusive in their representation of the student populations on campus during their "festival." On the night of the festival, as I walked through the gym and passed all of the beautifully decorated booths, I saw an over-representation of countries in Europe, a few Asian and Latinx countries, however, I did not see one booth that represented a country in Africa. Not one. How was it possible that during an international festival, in a school with a growing population of African American students and teachers, the festival managed to fail to include anything that represents the second largest continent on the planet?

Because my former administrators were not conscious of the misguided intentions of color blindness, they seemed to ignore that they had diverse students and faculty, and did not see the importance of including all of their peoples' histories and perspectives into the culture of the school. Schools seeking to be more authentic in their approaches to diversity cannot continue to be like the school I just mentioned and pat themselves on the back because they have a diverse staff or hosted a multicultural night on campus. They cannot be the campus that says they value diversity and inclusion, yet the histories, contributions, and perspectives of people of color are invisible in their everyday environments. As a teacher, taking a color blind stance helps no one see the needs of the diverse students in their care any clearer. Teachers must begin to think about this deeply held view amongst educators and administrators and all the implications of its existence in schools. Teachers must be willing to reflect on what they thought was best practice and be open to embracing practices that have proven to be even better. Color blindness and other culturally unaware ideologies and belief systems may seem enlightened and progressive on the surface. However, they are ultimately a shield enabling many to distance themselves from the painful realities of the past and hindering many from making sense of their effect on the present. Color blindness is an attempt to remove oneself from the hard work of overturning racial inequalities by pretending there are none. Unfortunately, the consequences of ignoring the significance of race in the classroom is directly connected to the failure in adequately educating the nation's diverse population of students.

From Color Blind to Color Conscious

The continued existence of the racial achievement gaps experienced by thousands of schools across the country is the number one indicator that current approaches to race in the classroom (or the avoidance of it) is not sufficient (Pang, 2018; Gay, 2010). Data collected from the National Center for Education Statistics stated that from 1992-2015 the reading achievement of White students continues to be higher than those of Black and Latinx students (NCES, 2017). The same can be said for math and science as well. Combine that with the disproportionate disciplinary outcomes and suspension rates for students of color, the effectiveness of the school-to-prison pipeline, and the unequal distribution of funds and resources to schools that house the poorest and diverse students make a strong case that something is not quite right (Logan & Oakley, 2012). The persistent lack of knowledge about these race-based inequalities in schools leaves well-intentioned educators ill-equipped to educate their diverse student populations and leaves millions of students of color in schools that are unable to tap into their unacknowledged potentials for academic greatness.

Educators that are interested in overturning unequal school outcomes for their culturally and linguistically diverse students must begin to interrupt and reverse these negative trends. For starters, teachers can begin the mental shift of color blindness in thinking that all students are mostly the same, and begin to embrace the challenge of becoming color-conscious. In becoming color-conscious, teachers should begin to acknowledge students' ethnic, racial, linguistic, and cultural differences in all aspects of their learning experiences. To do this, teachers need to not only recognize these differences but positively affirm them in schools. Teachers should seek to include more culturally diverse identities and perspectives in their curriculum. Teachers should provide all students with culturally diverse role models to emulate and revere in the pursuit of building good character traits among students.

Teachers should invest in increasing their cultural knowledge of the diverse students in their care to be fully equipped to embrace, educate, and include all the diverse knowledge, contributions, and ideas their students bring into the classroom. Being a color-conscious educator sends the message to students that who they are and where they come from is not only acknowledged, but valued and welcomed in today's classrooms and schools.

The differences in school experiences and outcomes for students in color-blind vs. color-conscious school environments are as significant as night and day. A perfect illustration of the effects of color-blind education and that of a color-conscious one can be seen in the 2013 documentary film, *American Promise*. In this film, which follows two African American boys, Seun and Idris, from kindergarten to college, gives audiences an intimate look at the school experiences of African American males in many public schools. Both boys begin their education careers at an elite majority White school in New York called Dalton. Both boys enter school excited and ready to learn; yet, shortly after their arrival, they begin to experience different treatment than their White counterparts. Both boys experienced behavior and academic difficulty. When their parents voiced concerns, they were met with disregard from teachers and constant recommendations for special education services for solutions. Even after Seun was diagnosed with dyslexia, his school experiences at Dalton seem only to get worse. His parents, unwilling to allow their son to be exposed to this kind of learning environment any longer, transferred him to the Benjamin Banneker Academy. It was a majority African American school. Idris remained at Dalton, and his educational experiences continued to spiral downward.

For Seun, Benjamin Banneker Academy became a life force in his academic career. His teachers, concerned with both his individual and cultural needs, provided him with learning experiences steeped in positive references to the strengths of African American culture, innovation, and achievement. He was taken on field trips to countries in Africa and was surrounded by educators of all backgrounds willing to commit to helping him through his dyslexia. They even played a vital role in helping him cope with the sudden accidental death of his little brother. Idris, on the other hand, in continuing his schooling at the elite Dalton, continued to experience marginalization and "otherness" at his school. At one point, he reflects about his experiences on camera by making a poignant, yet shared observation of many youth of color, "Would it be better if I were White?" Unfortunately, Idris' frustrations with the inequitable treatment at his school left him feeling as if his racial identity played a significant role in his disparaging experiences. For him, pondering the possibility of a more positive school experience if he were more like the other kids at school was tempting. Still, it would not have been better if Idris were White. It would have been better if the teachers and administrators at Dalton had taken into account the differences in histories, perspectives, experiences, and learning characteristics of African American males. It would have been better if Idris' teachers and administrators had not been color-blind in their diversity efforts and assumed all students learned the same. It would have been better if they not only sought to fill their schools physically with diverse students; they should have also tried to understand the needs and experiences those racial differences made in the school setting.

Addressing the dominance of color blind ideologies amongst teachers is critical to turning around the current inequitable school outcomes in lowered expectations, higher discipline rates, and disparities in special education referrals for marginalized students (NCES, 2017). Increasing teacher knowledge about the diverse histories, perspectives, and experiences of ethnically diverse students will help provide them with the foundation in creating more equitable school environments. Teachers can no longer afford to "treat all students the same." Every student is not the same. By continuing not to "see" the differences students bring into the classroom, teachers are choosing their comforts over those of the students. Failing to reconsider color-blind approaches is a fail in the attempts at authentic diversity and inclusion in the classroom. However, once teachers begin to understand and embrace the vital role that race and culture play in the creation of meaningful, relevant, and equitable learning experiences; teachers can begin to attain those characteristics and implement the strategies of truly culturally responsive educators.

Salandra Grice

CHAPTER 3

CULTURALLY RESPONSIVE TEACHING

"A hallmark of the culturally relevant notion of knowledge is that it is something that each student brings to the classroom. Students are not seen as empty vessels to be filled by all-knowing teachers. What they know is acknowledged, valued, and incorporated into the classroom."

–Gloria Ladson-Billings, *The Dreamkeepers*

There have been many arguments surrounding the cause of the racial achievement gaps in schools. These arguments range from lack of neighborhood quality, poverty, lack of parental involvement, to lack of educational values, just to name a few (Valencia, 2010). At first glance, these arguments sound valid and factually accurate. Many well-intentioned educators have found these reasons to be helpful in trying to pinpoint the source of failure for underachieving students of color and relieve themselves from the pressures of self-reflection. However, these culturally deficit reasonings do not help explain student failures; they only exacerbate them (Valencia, 2010). By blaming student failures on the student, their parents, their culture, or their neighborhood, teachers are exhibiting their failure in being conscious of historical, cultural, political, and socioeconomic factors that can affect poor and students of colors' academic success. In becoming a more conscious educator, teachers must be equipped with the knowledge of who their students are and where they come from. They must be knowledgeable of how socio-political, economic, and historical factors can affect their students' academic achievement. With this knowledge, teachers can help underachieving poor, and students of color become successful in their academic careers by empowering them with the tools necessary to overcome their circumstances. One of the most fundamental pedagogical approaches in achieving these goals is that of culturally responsive teaching.

What is Culturally Responsive Teaching?

Culturally responsive teaching is a general term for any teaching that uses the "cultural knowledge, prior experiences, frames of reference, and performance styles of ethnically diverse students to make learning encounters more relevant to and effective for them" (Gay, 2010, p. 31). Using teaching methods that incorporate a students' cultural background and frames of reference reverses the current trends in school culture that sees differences as deficits (or ignores them altogether in color blindness) and instead views these differences in a more positive light. The implementation of this teaching method can be done in many ways; however, educational researcher Geneva Gay summarized some key instructional aims which include the following:

> "...seeing cultural differences as assets; creating caring learning communities, where culturally different individuals and heritages are valued; using cultural knowledge of ethnically diverse cultures, families, and communities to guide curriculum development, classroom climates, instructional strategies, and relationships with students; challenging racial and cultural stereotypes, prejudices, racism, and other forms of intolerance, injustice, and oppression; being change agents for social justice and academic equity; mediating power imbalances in classrooms based on race, culture, ethnicity, and class; and accepting cultural responsiveness as endemic to educational effectiveness in all areas of learning for students from all ethnic groups" (Gay, 2010, p.31)

In classrooms, a culturally responsive approach rejects the empty vessel approach of filling students up with knowledge and takes into account and values what students already know. A culturally responsive approach makes sure that every student enters into a learning environment that is welcoming, accepting, and affirming of every aspect of their unique cultural identities. In practice, a culturally responsive reading teacher seeks to include multicultural literature that can reflect the lived experiences of students from diverse backgrounds. The culturally responsive writing teacher allows her students to share the stories passed down to them from their families and uses them to help translate into academic writing. Culturally responsive approaches in math use not only the images and contributions of Newton and Einstein, but also that of Benjamin Banneker, Dudley Woodard, Katherine Johnson, Alberto Calderon, and Mary G. Ross. Likewise, a culturally responsive science teacher would not only use the images and contributions of Benjamin Franklin and Charles Darwin, but they would also incorporate George Washington Carver, Marie Curie, Jane Goodall, Ellen Ochoa, Carlos Juan Finlay, and An Wang. Just like the math teacher, a culturally responsive science teacher uses scientific concepts to help students make sense of their world through curiosity and wonder, not the regurgitation of facts and assessments. Finally, the culturally responsive social studies or history teacher does not waste opportunities to make connections to the past by only asking students to memorize facts and dates. Instead, they take the opportunity to involve students in investigations and inquiry into the past.

Not only would a culturally responsive teacher include positive images of diverse achievers, but they would also provide meaningful and relevant learning experiences in which students could build on new math concepts by connecting it to their everyday lives. They would use historical events and figures such as George Washington and the Revolutionary War to understand the nation's beginnings, yet make sure to include multiple perspectives in these events as marginalized groups have had a very different experience in contributing to the building of this nation. A culturally responsive teacher uses those inquiries into the past to help students make sense of the present and become more active and engaged citizens in the future. A culturally responsive teacher doesn't teach to the test. A culturally responsive teacher seeks to create the most relevant, engaging, and academically challenging environment possible. A culturally responsive teacher thinks outside the box and takes educational risks. These risks involve developing more diverse ways of teaching and learning so that every student has a chance to learn in ways that are most relevant to them.

In order for teachers to create equitable and culturally responsive learning environments, they must understand the ethnically, linguistically, and culturally diverse histories and cultures of their students. They must increase their cultural knowledge. Understanding the culture of students is going to be a crucial element in culturally responsive teaching. However, when most teachers think of culture, they consistently refer to the basic levels of this complex force and too often only focus on food, clothing, holidays, or festivals. In doing so, teachers shortchange not only the students whose cultures are reduced to foods and festivities, but every student misses the opportunity to get a deeper understanding of the diverse classmates around them. While food and holiday celebrations can be used as unifying experiences among students, they cannot be the method by which teachers employ multicultural education and culturally responsive teaching into the classroom. So, what is culture anyway?

What is Culture?

In his 2010 thought-provoking book *Why Race and Culture Matter in Schools*, Tyrone C. Howard describes culture as "a complex constellation of values, mores, norms, customs, ways of being, ways of knowing, and traditions that provides a general design for living, is passed from generation to generation, and serves as a pattern for interpreting reality" (p.51). In short, culture is something that we all have, and it informs the way we view and interact with the world. Culture is so complex that we cannot just sum it up into superficial elements that we can see, hear, taste, touch, wear, or eat. We must begin to think of culture as a "system rather than a list of aspects of life" (Pang, 2018, p. 45).

To comprehend these complexities, cultural researchers have described culture by dividing it into a series of components or levels. These levels of culture are useful in helping teachers understand the fullness of what consists of culture and open the door to educators growing their knowledge of the different ways of thinking, acting, and believing among their students (Pang, 2018). A representation of these levels and the components that they consist of are represented in Figure 1.

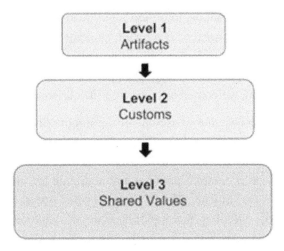

Figure 1. Levels of Culture

The first level, artifacts, is the most basic and tangible level. At this level are elements such as language, dances, holidays, myths, folktales, and history. Level two, customs, can include tone of voice, phrases, nonverbal cues, greetings, conversational patterns and gender roles. Level three, shared values, can include beliefs, norms, and expectations. It also consists of values such as religious beliefs, fears, laws, and expectations (Pang, 2018). Teachers must reflect upon, and ask themselves, how familiar they are with the different levels of culture within which their students may interact. Are teachers only fluent in the smallest and most artificial aspects of students' culture, or are they also aware of the larger and deeper aspects as well? Teachers may think that their good intentions in having their students read a book on Cinco de Mayo are sufficient for the inclusion of cultural diversity in the classroom; but if one cannot pinpoint the unseen cultural norms, values, expectations, and beliefs of their linguistically and ethnically diverse students, then teachers are not including enough cultural aspects. A sufficient inclusion of students' culture would be taking into consideration the communal interaction styles of Latinx and African American students and allowing opportunities for them to work cooperatively in groups. A sufficient inclusion of students' culture would be building trusting relationships with students and parents by inviting them into the classroom to share about the importance of cultural and historical celebrations. This type of inclusion can be done through presentations, interviews, and read-alouds conducted by and with students and their parents. As a result, students will feel a sense of pride and acceptance in being able to share important aspects of their lives with their classmates. Parents will also feel part of their children's learning experiences by being welcomed as experts in the classroom.

When teachers are not conscious of the important role culture plays in the lives of their students or what the culture of their students consists of, they can inadvertently push their own cultural norms onto their students and create a disconnect in creating positive and authentic learning environments for culturally diverse students. This disconnect often occurs when the culture of the teacher or school is incompatible with the cultures of the diverse students it interacts with. There is usually a lack of a bridge between the two. One of the clearest examples I can share in regards to this conflict is in the case of different communication patterns between White teachers and students and teachers of color. As previously mentioned, one of the more significant aspects of culture includes communication patterns. In my experience as a teacher of color, I have noticed a vast difference in the way White teachers interpret the communication patterns of their students, parents, and colleagues of color.

Communication between any two individuals can sometimes be tricky when one or the other misinterprets the meanings of the other person's tone, facial expressions, mannerisms, or use of language. In cross-cultural communications, the margin for misinterpretation is increased, especially when either party is unfamiliar or has negative assumptions about the communication patterns of the culturally different person they are engaging with. The countless instances of the tone-policing, feeling "threatened," and volume control projected onto me during conversations is always an indication that the person I am talking to is making those assumptions on my behalf. The often passionate, animated, or direct manner in which many African American women communicate can be a stark contrast to the soft, stoic, matter-of-fact, and passive way that many White women communicate. The media-driven illustration of the harshness of the "angry" Black woman often pits these two different styles against one another instead of building a bridge of understanding in different communication patterns. Such a bridge would have been helpful in my teaching career during one particular interaction between myself and another colleague who was White.

This particular interaction began during dismissal when a White colleague of mine begins to yell for me to walk my line of students faster. I made no reply to this teacher as I was in the middle of getting my students home in a safe manner. She, however, had more to say. As I prepared to leave the gym after dismissing my students, this teacher yelled across the gym, "Hey, Kinder, it's your turn to stay!" Because it was my first year at the school and the beginning of the school year, I was unaware of any rotation for dismissal duty. I replied that I didn't know and asked if there was a schedule that I could follow in the future. This simple request for some structure during dismissal procedures was met with ridicule and contempt. As I walked back to my classroom to leave for the day, I overheard the teacher talking about my request for a schedule with another teacher. Apparently, my need for a schedule was pure comedy, and the slow pace of my students was more than this teacher could bear. She didn't realize I was right behind her.

As I approached, I said to her and her accomplice, "If anyone has an issue with the amount of time it takes 50 plus kinders to walk to the buses, I am more than open to suggestions on how to get them there more quickly." This simple but direct approach to her passive communication style sets off a chain of events straight out of a 90s high school drama. Later, when this teacher gave her version of events to the principal, she repeatedly claimed that I aggressively yelled at her during our interaction. To this teacher, whose preference for communicating was passive aggressive; my direct style may have felt aggressive and loud to her. People in cross-cultural communication situations can sometimes develop "selective perceptions" of those they are in dialogue with especially if the other participant represents a racial group they do not have positive feelings towards or prior authentic interactions with (Koppelman, 2017).

This selective perception of angry or aggressive communication on behalf of people of color, particularly Black females, is a phenomenon experienced by teachers of color across the nation (Morrison, 2019). I am not the first teacher of color to have her character misrepresented due to someone else's uninformed assumptions, fears, and lack of authentic communication experience with those different than themselves. As annoying as these instances of miscommunication are when they happen to educators, for students, they have more serious consequences. When teachers do not have a firm grasp of the cultures and communication styles of their students, teachers often project lower expectations and in turn discipline more harshly and more often students of color, than their White counterparts (T.C. Howard, 2010). Many of these discipline problems teachers say they are experiencing with students of color are often based on subjective interpretations of what the teacher feels is non-compliant or disrespectful. Many teachers do not understand that many students come from homes where parents often communicate in straightforward manners. Unfortunately, many teachers expect students to know what they want them to do even when it is communicated passively. It can be challenging for students of color (particularly Black students) to view authority in a teacher who presents him/herself as passive or mousy. It was always tricky for me as well. To bridge this gap, teachers must gain more authentic experience in communicating with those that are different from themselves. In other words, to be a culturally responsive teacher, teachers must be able to mediate between their students' cultures and the culture of the school and bridge the gap when inconsistencies between the two arise (Gay, 2010). To some, becoming fluent in another language seems daunting; however, many teachers already have practice in this area whether they realize it or not.

Historically, teachers have already taught in culturally responsive ways in schools. Unfortunately, the only cultures schools have been responsive to have been "Eurocentric, male-oriented, English-speaking, heterosexist, and middle-class" (T.C. Howard, 2010, p. 56). This may surprise many teachers because of the way Eurocentric norms have been seamlessly woven into every fabric of most school experiences. For many, the culture in schools may seem "normal," "right," or "just the way things are." The preference for all things Eurocentric is continuously transmitted in the way that the curriculum that is taught, books that are read, history that is the content focus, and communication and interaction styles that are valued. This can create school cultures that run counter to the home cultures of students whose backgrounds are different from the White, mainstream norms demonstrated and expected of them in schools. As a result, those aforementioned cultural conflicts can and do ensue. Culturally relevant values, histories, communication styles, hair, and clothing can become weapons to admonish and discipline students who do not present themselves in ways deemed acceptable in Eurocentric schools. Braids and Afros become inappropriate, long hair on boys is a distraction, students of color simply gathering to talk in the hallways between classes are seen as troublemakers, home languages are forbidden because students must speak proper English, and students standing up for themselves in the face of unfairness are seen as challenging authority. It can be very discouraging to come to a learning environment that rejects who students are at every turn.

Teachers must reflect on how they would feel in an atmosphere that sent messages to them daily that how they looked, spoke, and dressed was not welcomed, and one must change in order to be accepted. If teachers want students to have more positive school experiences, they must become more accepting of the various and diverse cultures that students come to school with. Teachers must begin to value and accept more than one way of dressing, speaking, and combing one's hair. They must dive deeper into the cultures of diverse students to get a better understanding of their values, beliefs, and ways of knowing and being. Educators must get out of their comfort zone of only interacting with those like themselves and begin to see what life is like for other people. Teachers must become more culturally competent and be open to immersing themselves in the experiences of others.

When I lived in Singapore, I got first-hand experience of what it was like to be immersed in a different culture. The cultural ways of thinking, acting, and being among Singaporeans were very different compared to that of Americans. There was no such thing as personal space. They believe that items were to be passed between two people with two hands, not one. There were different safety expectations in transporting children; car seats were optional. There were different ways to get on and ride escalators; stay to the right. However, the most jarring difference I experienced was how they worshipped at church.

Although Singapore is a majority Muslim country, we were able to quickly find a great Christian church not far from our apartment. However, even though the majority Chinese-Singaporean congregants and I were worshipping the same God, we had different ways of expressing that worship. I had never been to such a quiet church service in all my life! There was no clapping, no shouting, no talking to the preacher, just silence. It was quite an adjustment from the majority Black Methodist and Baptist churches I attended in the states. Nonetheless, it was a great experience to be able to interact with people who were different from me in such an intimate setting. Although it was not my preference for silence during worship, I had greater respect for their cultural ways of thinking, acting, and being. Having that weekly exposure to a culturally different atmosphere, I could respect their culturally different expressions instead of fearing or ridiculing them for it. However, just because a group of people can display specific cultural characteristics does not mean that those characteristics will be true for everyone in that group. Teachers can get a more accurate and authentic look into the lives of their diverse students by conducting cultural immersions into the lives of their students. By attending community events, making home visits, or simply sitting down to chat with students during the day, teachers can gain transformational knowledge of the authentic values and beliefs of students. A little more effort towards building more authentic understandings around cultural differences can go a long way in providing more welcoming and inclusive classroom environments.

A People's History Approach to Student Diversity

Educator and scholar Geneva Gay (2010) puts it best when she cautions educators about stereotyping when cultivating cultural responsiveness in her trailblazing work in *Culturally Responsive Teaching: Theory, Research, and Practice*. She states that in discussing common characteristics among groups of people, it "does not imply that they will be identically manifested by all group members. Nor will these characteristics be negated if some group members do not exhibit any of them as described" (p.10). Any future reference to characteristics displayed by a group of people is simply that, characteristics. People are still individuals, and many factors create variables (such as gender, class, age, and sexual orientation) to the degree in which these characteristics may be displayed. Teachers must be knowledgeable of all of the diversity within the cultures of diverse students. They cannot rely on simple stereotypes in their understandings of others.

To accomplish this, teachers interested in becoming conscious educators must reflect on their knowledge of the histories, perspectives, and cultures of major groups in America which include (but are not limited to) African, Latinx, Native, and Asian American peoples. Furthermore, teachers must also assess their attitudes and views of the cultures of African, Latinx, Native, and Asian American peoples as well. If teacher knowledge consists mainly of the food, clothing, music, holidays, and a few (if any) mainstream famous figures, this demonstrates a typical (albeit) superficial understanding of cultures different from themselves. If teacher reflections on their attitudes bring up feelings that reflect a perceived inferior, barbaric, abnormal, or "otherness" about these groups, they too, are exhibiting a common, yet devalued feeling regarding people different from themselves as well. These attitudes and understandings among educators must be evaluated and addressed. If teachers only want to understand linguistically and ethnically diverse students on superficial levels and maintain the low expectations that are already projected onto them, then no further reflection is needed. However, if teachers want to become more culturally aware and responsive educators, then they are going to have to delve a little deeper into the histories of diverse students in order to gain a deeper understanding of the cultures the students come from. The task of increasing teacher knowledge about those histories is going to require a little effort on behalf of educators.

An increased and intentional effort to learn more about diverse cultures and histories is needed because it has become painfully apparent that the current methods used to teach history in today's public schools have failed the general public miserably. Evidence that there is a severe lack of understanding about the history of America is all too easy to find. My experiences in attempting to guide teachers to include more diverse perspectives on historical events are often met with strong resistance or apathy. Historian and educator James Loewen (2011) have also lamented his experiences in assessing teachers' knowledge and attitudes about history in America. One of the most telling instances he recalls is the depth of the lack of understanding many teachers have in regards to the circumstances surrounding one of the most pivotal events in American history, the Civil War. According to Loewen, many teachers falsely believe that the Civil War was caused by a dispute over states' rights, not the well-documented debate over the enslavement of Africans in America and the desire to expand this profitable yet inhumane institution across America. This fundamental misunderstanding in the cause of such a polarizing event has had devastating consequences on teachers and students' abilities to make connections from this nation's racially oppressive past to its continued racially oppressive and hostile present.

Thankfully, curriculum changes are coming down the pipeline (at least in some states) to help teachers fill in those gaps of knowledge amongst their students. The Texas State Board of Education recently released a statement regarding changes to their history curriculum saying that students will now learn that slavery played a "central role" in the cause of the Civil War (Mosbergen, 2018). The often-cited reason for the Civil War as a simple matter of "state's rights" has left many unable to think critically about this country's deliberate dedication to introduce, maintain, and expand the institution of chattel slavery by any means necessary, even if it means war. This change in perspective will be crucial in helping future students make connections from America's slave past and its continued effects on race relations in America. This change will be a significant mind shift for many who were under the impression that America was built on liberty and justice for all. It is a significant shift nonetheless. Unfortunately, more shifts in the perceptions of the history of America are needed in more areas than this. A multicultural and multiple perspectives approach to understanding history will give educators the necessary foundation of the complexity of events and issues that have shaped, molded, and ultimately continue to affect how diverse people live, act, and adapt to the continued racial inequalities experienced today. This approach to increase teacher knowledge about the cultures of their diverse students will help teachers to no longer see their diverse students for what they lack in Eurocentric norms and values, but instead help them understand the value, contributions, and resilience of their cultures that they already possess.

Filling in the Gaps

How much knowledge does the average teacher possess regarding the histories and cultures of Native and Indigenous groups in America? Due to their almost complete absence in many mainstream history textbooks and classrooms, not very much. Historically, Native American or Indigenous peoples have the longest and consequently, one of the most tragic histories in America. Anthropologists and historical researchers all point to Native and

Indigenous peoples as the first inhabitants of America whose cultures, customs, and traditions have contributed significantly to the making and maintaining of the modern American culture we have today. From the help of the Wampanoags given to the first Pilgrims at Plymouth Rock to the foundations of the U.S. government borrowed from the Iroquois League, there are not many facets of American society that cannot be traced back to Native culture (Pang, 2018). Unfortunately, if one were to ask any number of teachers and students what their knowledge of Native cultures and societies consists of one would undoubtedly get references to tomahawks, feathered headdresses, moccasins, Thanksgiving, Pocahontas, Squanto, and maybe even Sacagawea. Another unfortunate side effect of the lack of knowledge surrounding Native and Indigenous cultures is that many teachers still refer to students and people from these diverse groups of people as "Indians." The practice of doing so is culturally insensitive and geographically incorrect, as Native Americans are not from India. Furthermore, it reduces their vast and diverse cultural groups of many peoples and many languages to a centuries-old misinformed stereotype that they have tried desperately (through education and activism) to reverse.

Not only do teachers and students know little about the people of Native American ancestry, but many may not have very positive feelings about them either. Due to many people's lack of engagement in authentic relationships with people different from themselves, negative assumptions have gone unchecked. Because of the incessant negative, inaccurate, incomplete, and racist portrayals by textbooks (we'll dive into that later), literature, movies, the arts and music, Native Americans have been reduced to savage, uncivilized, relics of the past in many people's minds (Brayboy & Searle, 2007). The result of all of this lack of knowledge and negative portrayals of Native peoples in our nation's public schools has resulted in achievement rates that resemble disproportionately high rates of below basic performances in math and reading for many Native students (T.C. Howard, 2010). This is unacceptable and deserves an action-based solution.

These actions include increasing teachers' knowledge. Once teachers begin to increase their knowledge about the diverse and complex histories of Native and Indigenous peoples, they will learn of the well-established nations of the Mohawk, Oneida, Onondaga, Cayuga, and Seneca that lived thousands of years before Columbus set foot in what is now America (Pang, 2018). They will know that after the arrival of Europeans, the livelihoods of Native cultures began to deteriorate in vast numbers. This cultural genocide decimated the Arawak, Taino, Patuxet, and Karankawa, among others; and before the end of the nineteenth century there would only be 250,000 Native peoples as opposed to the estimated 18 million pre-Columbus Native population (Pang, 2018). Since then, Native peoples have been in ongoing struggles to maintain their land (after numerous broken treaties), and maintain their way of life after forced attempts at assimilation failed (National Museum of the American Indian, 2016). Once teachers begin to understand Native history, they may begin to understand why many do not celebrate Thanksgiving because it reminds many of the genocide of their people, which that holiday represents. Once teachers dig deeper into the lives of Native students, they will no longer hold them up as hyper-visible characters of the past all the while making invisible their present-day struggles and contributions (Brayboy & Searle, 2007).

In order for teachers to learn more authentic and complete history about Native and Indigenous students, I recommend a self-directed history lesson that will include books, films, documentaries, and websites created by and about Native peoples. I would begin with books like *Bury My Heart at Wounded Knee* by Dee Brown and *An Indigenous Peoples' History of the United States* by Roxanne Dunbar-Ortiz. I would continue with films like *Dawnland* and *In Whose Honor? American Indian Mascots in Sports*. I would frequent websites like the National Museum of American Indian at www.nmai.si.edu and the National Indian Education Association at www.niea.org, just to name a few. I hope that the teachers who take the time to view or read any of the information presented in these resources will walk away with a greater understanding and appreciation of the sacrifice, contribution, and resilience of Native American peoples. The same should be done with other student groups as well.

What do everyday teachers know and understand about the unique histories and experiences of their African American students? The history of African Americans in the U.S. is arguably the most contested one. The mere mention of African American history can bring about many images and feelings of inferiority, degradation, subjugation, fear, resentment, shame, guilt, anger, and overall disgust from those not only outside the community, but inside as well. They are dynamic, complex, and complicated people. If teachers are honest with themselves in reflecting on their attitudes toward their African American students and their families, they may be able to identify with some, maybe even all of those feelings, if they are honest. My personal experiences as an African American have revealed the way many of these negative feelings manifest themselves in society and classrooms as well.

Teachers looking to become more culturally responsive to the African American students in their class must begin to unravel the complicated and ongoing history of Africans in America for themselves. In doing so, one must begin before the period of enslavement. For a people whose beginnings coincide with the beginnings of humanity, it is very peculiar how any discussion surrounding African American history doesn't begin in Africa. If teachers can begin there, they will begin to understand how African culture, innovation, medicine, and education are the foundations for all that is looked to in the Greek and Latin educational paradigms referenced today (Smith, 1998). For example, the first alphabet was created by Egyptians. Imhotep, an Egyptian Chancellor to the Pharaoh was credited as the great architect of the pyramids and a great man of medicine, too. However, Egypt was not the only great African country to pave the way in innovations. The present-day countries of Ethiopia, Sudan, and others in West Africa also founded great kingdoms as far back as 3,000 B.C. up until the 1600s that could boast of incredible wealth and knowledge that was known to other great nations such as Greece and China (De Villiers & Sheila, 2007). Africa was never the "dark continent" that those who sought to exploit it reduced it to in order to seize all it had. Africans have always made significant contributions to the world. It's about time all students understand that it was not slaves that were stolen from Africa; but doctors, scientists, artists, architects, and educators.

Even when looking at the legacy of slavery in the U.S. which officially began in 1619, African Americans can be credited for giving all they had (including their literal bodies) to building the U.S. into what it is today. From the building of the White House, major colleges and universities, to the number of inventions, movements, music, language, food, and pop cultural phenomenon, they have been at the helms of creation in all that is America.

Sadly, too many teachers in too many schools across America are only familiar with a fraction of that knowledge. That small fraction typically is given to students in decontextualized broken pieces with no connection to the current state of Black America today. It may be mixed in with a few brief shout outs to Martin Luther King, Jr. and Rosa Parks, all while proclaiming a false call to color blindness. These same individuals will likely argue that slavery happened a long time ago, it was evil, but it has no relevance to the state of race relations in the country today. If only it were that simple. To truly get a better understanding of what the culture of African Americans is like, what they value, and what their perspectives are, the ugly parts of U.S. history so many teachers would like to forget must be discussed. Unfortunately, for the people whose ancestors and families survived one of the worst holocausts in world history and are still struggling to overturn the racist justifications that ushered it in, it is something *that can never be forgotten.* Abolitionist, orator, and former slave, Frederick Douglass summed up the necessity of understanding the impact of America's practice of slavery in a speech he ironically was asked to give during a Fourth of July celebration (before emancipation). He states that "There is not a nation on the earth guilty of practices, more shocking and bloody, than are the people of these United States" (1852). We have yet to reckon with that past.

However, any delve into the history of slavery in America should not be done to shame or to make the descendants of former enslavers feel guilty. Although feelings of guilt, anger, and shame are common in these discussions, such is not the goal. Instead, the study and teaching of the enslavement of Africans in America must be done not only through a lens of truth; but also triumph, resilience, and resistance of African American people. Even though African Americans suffered significant losses through the separation of their families, removal of their heritage, and the denial of their humanity through torture and forced labor, still, they rise (thanks Maya Angelou). It should be understood that African Americans did not take slavery lying down or without a fight and worked together with White, Latinx, and Jewish allies and abolitionists and even reluctant presidents to gain their freedom. More accurate and complete history in schools will teach students that their struggle was not over even after emancipation. The following decades up until today still include the fight for racial equality for African Americans in the United States. Government policies that continue to target the progress of African Americans by discriminating against them in the areas of housing, healthcare, employment, and education continue to disproportionally affect the African American community. They are continuously fighting for their right to equal protection under the law by resisting all forms of police violence. There is no doubt that African Americans will continue to fight these same fights towards equality even when many are too afraid even to confront them.

In order for teachers to learn a more authentic and complete history of African American students, I recommend more self-directed history lessons that include books, films, documentaries, and websites created by and about African American peoples. I would begin with books like *Invisible Man* by Ralph Ellison and *The Souls of Black Folk* by W.E.B. DuBois. I would continue with films like *Eyez on the Prize, Malcolm X,* and *13th.* I would frequent websites like the National Museum of African American History and Culture at www.nmaahc.si.edu and the Schomburg Center for Research in Black Culture at www.nypl.org/about/locations/schomburg, just to name a few. I hope that the teachers who take the time to view or read any of the information presented in these resources will also walk away with a greater understanding and appreciation of the sacrifice, contribution, and resilience of African American peoples.

The history of Latinx Americans has also been one of similar (if not intertwined) struggle and triumph with Native and African Americans. Teachers should pause to reflect on their knowledge of the many diverse peoples of Latinx descent and their many contributions. Paul Ortiz (2018) recounts in his epic reimagining of Latinx history in *An African American and Latinx American History of the United States* that if one is looking for the roots of America's democratic society one must look to Latinx America, the Caribbean, and Africa as well as Europe. Just as much, any discussion of Mexican history in America cannot be done without the intertwined heritages of African, Indigenous, and European influences. Because of the vast and varied lineages of Latinx peoples, I cannot do them all justice within the context of this short introduction. However, I can point in the right direction when discussing Latinx America's history within the U.S.

Just as one should not start African American history with slavery, one should not start Latinx history there either. Indigenous peoples in Mexico thrived for thousands of years before European contact. The Aztecs, Olmecs, Mayans and other nations were very advanced in agriculture, science, and astronomy well before Spain arrived. The Mayans even created a calendar that was designed 1,000 years before the European Gregorian Calendar used today (Pang, 2018). Historian Ivan Van Sertima (1976) even documents the travels of Africans to the Americas (before Columbus) in the preservation of Olmec statues found in Mexico that resemble African faces. The mingling of these different groups only became more prominent after the introduction of the European slave trade. As a result, by the end of its height during the 19th century, African, Latinx, and Indigenous peoples would become intertwined not only in their cultures but also in their fights for freedom.

The intersection of Mexico's War of Independence from Spain in 1821 and the American belief in Manifest Destiny played a significant role in the literal shaping of the United States. After many territorial battles in Texas and the signing of the Treaty of Guadalupe Hidalgo in 1848, the U.S. won its fight to expand its slave territories, and the Indigenous Mexicans in California, Utah, Texas, Nevada, Arizona, Colorado and more were now U.S. citizens (Pang, 2018). Many of the U.S.'s struggles with Mexico stemmed from the anti-slavery approach of many Mexican leaders such as Jose Maria Morelos, Miguel Hidalgo, and Vicente Guerrero. All of whom looked to the revolutionaries of Haiti, such as Toussaint L'Ouverture for revolutionary inspiration (Ortiz, 2018).

Even though Mexican Americans newly acquired citizenship offered them land and religious rights, it did not come without discrimination (Pang, 2018). Back in Mexico, political conflicts after the Mexican War with Spain sent many Mexicans looking for work in America. This struggle to provide would expose Mexican workers to deplorable wages and working conditions and spark numerous strikes and political uprisings aimed at alleviating these conditions for not only Mexicans, but Puerto Ricans, Cubans, and Dominicans as well. Many revolutionaries would emerge during these struggles as many looked to the leadership of Francisco (Pancho) Villa, Emiliano Zapata, Cesar Chavez, Dolores Huerta, and Philip Vera Cruz, just to name a few. As mentioned earlier, Latinx Americans struggle intertwined with Native and African Americans as they too, fought against segregation, endured racial violence during the Zoot Suit Riots, and have continued to fight for full citizenship throughout the U.S.'s changes in immigration reform. Mexican Americans and all Latinx Americans continue the fight for full citizenship and equality in the United States to this day.

In order for teachers to learn more authentic and complete history about Latinx American students, I recommend continued self-directed history lessons that include books, films, documentaries, and websites created by and about Latinx American peoples. I would begin with books like *Race and Class in the Southwest* by Mario Barrera and *Between Two Worlds: Mexican Immigrants in the United States* by David Gutierrez. I would continue with films like *Precious Knowledge, Children of the Fields,* and *Harvest of Shame.* I would frequent websites like the National Museum of the American Latino at www.americanlatinomuseum.org/. I hope that the teachers who take the time to view or read any of the information presented in these resources will also walk away with a greater understanding and appreciation of the sacrifice, contribution, and resilience of Latinx American peoples.

What about the histories and experiences of Asian and Pacific Islander students? The history of Asians in America has somewhat of a different tone in that even though they carry some of the same scars from discrimination and stereotypes that other groups of color do, Asian Americans have the double-edge of carrying the "model" stereotype (if there was one) above all other ethnic groups. However, like other people of color, it didn't start out that way. Their history in America began after slavery officially ended in 1865 when there was a new need for a cheap labor force. Chinese immigrants soon began an increase in arriving in California to work in the goldfields in the west. Soon after their arrival, their success drew criticism from White Americans and the Chinese became the first immigrants to be prohibited from migration with the Chinese Exclusion Act of 1882 (Takaki, 2008; Pang, 2018). Other discriminatory practices were also upheld that prevented Asian Americans from owning land and restricted their children to segregated schools (Pang, 2018). However, the Chinese were not the only ones who suffered.

Japanese Americans arrived around the same time also in search of bettering their condition through economic success in America. Unfortunately, they too suffered through perilous events in history, including racism, discrimination, and internment. This period of internment, the state-sanctioned practice of removing Japanese American citizens from their homes after Pearl Harbor, was ushered in by President Franklin D. Roosevelt. The justification for this mistreatment was based only on the fact that they were of Japanese descent. As a result, over 120,000 Japanese Americans were affected by this removal. Forty years later, President Reagan would sign the Civil Liberties Act of 1988, and it would be the first time the U.S. not only apologized but compensated a group of people whose rights had been taken away (Pang, 2018). Read that last line one more time.

However, soon after things began to change for Asian Americans and Ellen D. Wu (2014) chronicles the transformation of Asian Americans ascension from the "yellow peril" and "pig-tailed coolies" of the nineteenth century to the poster people for how to "make it" in America. This shift in the perception of Asian Americans is summed up by Wu (2014) as a political strategy when she states:

"Recognizing that the Asian Pacific region loomed large on the U.S. foreign relations agenda, community representatives strategically typecast themselves, asserting that their own ancestries endowed them with innate cultural expertise that qualified them to serve as the United States' most natural ambassadors to the Far East. Therefore, they suggested, admitting people of Japanese and Chinese heritage to first-class citizenship made good diplomatic sense" (p. 5).

This political hoist did not come without consequences as this boost for the Asian American came at a price many African and Latinx Americans are still paying for today. As their disparities in the lack of social mobility are looked at as cultural depravity, this simplistic and racist stereotype fails to take into account the lack of systemic advantage that it is. I have often heard the phrase "Asians overcame their discrimination; why can't Blacks?" Without the understanding of how the ascension of Asian Americans in society has been a combined effort of revised public policy, revamped public perceptions, and cultural ingenuity, it can be easy to come to such a conclusion (Wu, 2014). Understanding how America institutionally "stopped being racist" towards Asian Americans is a careful consideration (and often missing piece) in understanding the differences in social outcomes between them and other marginalized groups (Wu, 2014). However, even this seemingly good stereotype does not always work in favor of those it is projected onto as it distorts and ignores the diversity of experiences within Asian American and Pacific Islander groups. One cannot stereotype the Asian experience as one of absolute success and mobility as many Korean, Vietnamese, Laotian, Hmong, and other groups often experience harrowing levels of poverty, academic failure, and dropout rates similar to that of African, Native, and Latinx American groups (Pang, 2018; Joo, Reeves, & Rodrigue, 2016). Painting all Asian and Pacific Islander groups with the broad brush of the "model minority" often hurts the students and families suffering from these experiences as many do not get the support they need to overcome these circumstances (Lew, 2007).

In order for teachers to learn more authentic and complete history about Asian American students, I recommend continued self-directed history lessons that include books, films, documentaries, and websites created by and about Asian and Pacific Islander American peoples. I would begin with books like *Strangers from a Different Shore* by Ronald Takaki and *The Color of Success: Asian Americans and the Making of the Model Minority* by Ellen D. Wu. I would continue with films like *Farewell to Manzanar* and *Hollywood Chinese.* I would also frequent websites like the Japanese American National Museum at www.janm.org and the Smithsonian Asian Pacific American Center at www.smithsonianapa.org/. Again, I hope that the teachers who take the time to view or read any of the information presented in these resources will also walk away with a greater understanding and appreciation of the sacrifice, contribution, and resilience of Asian and Pacific Islander American peoples.

Please note that it is not always necessary (however helpful) to read "insider" sources; there are many notable historians and scholars such as Howard Zinn and James Loewen that could also help fill in any gaps in understanding regarding diverse peoples as well. To help students, teachers can access a plethora of multicultural children's books for all ages from authors such as Faith Ringgold, Alma Flor Ada, Grace Lin, and Chief Jake Swamp. There are also many historical websites created by people of color such as Blackpast.org and Cradleboard.org for the sole purpose of educating the masses about their people, from their perspectives. Museums are also a great source of information and can give profound insights into little known historical facts and histories and how it connects everyone to the foundations of this country's origins. To be clear, teachers are not to aim to create classrooms that are reflective of every single student's culture, but instead are to "recognize when there is a problem for a particular child and how to seek its cause in the most broadly conceived fashion" (Delpit, 2006, p. 167). Problems such as intolerance, exclusion, and lack of representation of culturally and ethnically diverse students can all be remedied with the gaining of increased knowledge amongst teachers. Educators that become conscious of the histories, heritages, cultures, and characteristics of their linguistically and ethnically diverse students are going to be better able to incorporate more culturally responsive teaching practices. They will be able to use the knowledge of their students' home cultures, values, and perspectives to help make more accurate and inclusive curriculum choices and more culturally congruent delivery methods of that content. They will be able to obtain an overall improved classroom environment to be one that is not merely tolerant of racial and cultural diversity, but actually embraces and affirms it. In other words, when culturally responsive teachers "are able to make connections between the cultural knowledge, beliefs, and practices that students bring from home, and the content and pedagogy that they use in their classrooms, the academic performance and overall schooling experiences of learners from culturally diverse groups will improve" (T.C. Howard, 2010, p. 69). This is a goal I hope every teacher seeks to obtain.

Poor and Low Income

Not only can understanding the ethnic and cultural backgrounds of students transform their achievement rates, but having a firm understanding of how the histories that surround these cultures have influenced the socioeconomic status of many students of color. Conscious educators understand that students who come from poor and low socioeconomic neighborhoods did not create those neighborhoods on their own. There is no "culture of poverty" as some social scientists, and some high-profile educators would have us believe (Pang, 2018; Gorski, 2019). Poverty is only the direct manifestation of the effects of inequality and lack of opportunity in people's lives. One cannot just will themselves out of it. To overturn these injustices, structural systems which control the opportunities for economic advancement must be redesigned for equity. This is no secret as research by numerous sociologists points to the fact that even the poorest and most urban neighborhoods only reflect their intentional design (Wells et al., 2012). In the groundbreaking book, *The Color of Law*, Richard Rothstein (2017) carefully illustrates how America's long-standing discriminatory and racist housing policies have been the catalyst in deteriorating neighborhoods of color for decades. When educators are conscious of the socioeconomic contexts that their students emerge from, they are better able to understand that student failure is not merely happening because of a defect in the student but multiple factors including poverty can impact student achievement.

The idea that the environment or "place" can profoundly shape the opportunities that students experience has been echoed throughout research for decades (Johnson, 2012). When students' experiences are steeped in various levels of poverty and depravity, it plays a significant role in how it affects student achievement. Some students are affected by these outcomes in more ways than others. Many of these differences fall along racial and ethnic lines. Recent statistics show that 21 percent of students live in poverty; of that total, 38 percent are African American, 35 percent are Native American, and 32 percent are Latinx (Pang, 2018). Research on the effects of poverty on student achievement produced revealed that students of color who live in poverty are severely isolated from the opportunities and experiences many middle-class and affluent students are accustomed to. The "opportunity structure" that evades communities of color keeps resources, knowledge, and dominant cultural norms which are essential to navigating school and the workforce at bay. This lack of exposure has resulted in the continuous and vicious cycle of a lack of opportunity in their lives (Galster, 2012). Educators cannot afford to continue to "blame the victim" in hopes that poor students will pull themselves up by their bootstraps and try just harder. Teachers need to be able to fill in any gaps of knowledge, so students are more likely to succeed in a world dominated by people and norms outside their own. Like any organism seeking life and prosperity, the proper environment that supports the growth and needs of its host is essential.

As a former kindergarten teacher, one of my students' favorite science units was on the plant life cycle. During this unit, students not only discussed what plants are, whether they were living or nonliving, but they also discussed what plants needed in order for them to grow. To illustrate the importance of plants having everything they need like sunlight, soil, water, air, and space to grow, students conducted a series of experiments. They took four lima bean seeds and planted each one with a significant need for its growth missing. One was planted in soil and given sunlight but lacked water. One was planted in soil, given water, but lacked sunlight. One was given water and sunlight but lacked soil. The last one was given all three significant needs of water, soil, and sunlight, but it lacked air in that it was zipped up inside of a plastic baggie. Finally, they planted the fifth seed with everything it needed and in the right proportions to be able to compare it to the growth of the others. Students were then asked to make predictions regarding how they thought each seed would fare under each condition, and then they waited.

Each day, students were asked to observe and record the changes in each of the seeds planted. To their surprise, the seeds that did not get everything they needed to grow and thrive differed in their growth rates from the seed that had everything it needed. Such is the same for many students. Many educators with students from low-income (or otherwise) homes suffering from some significant degree of lack do not realize that many of these students struggle because they do not have all that they need. It's time for a mind shift in the way many teachers view their poor and low-income students. Continuing to use victim-blaming or deficit induced explanations for the lack of achievement many low-income student's experience is no longer acceptable, nor logical. Teachers must understand that yes, some students are coming from home situations that are less than desirable. However, many teachers miss the opportunity to see the strengths that many students come to school with in spite of less than perfect home lives. How much more difficult are teachers making achievement for students when instead of seeing the value of the knowledge, culture, and experiences students do have, they create unnecessary hurdles by reducing their efforts with and expectations of students in poverty? Deficit thinking in the mind of the educator is the kryptonite to student success.

Imagine if while conducting the plant experiments, I had tried to explain the lack of growth of some of the plants by using many of the deficit-oriented excuses many teachers provide about their low-income students.

Imagine if I tried to explain to my students the reason some of the plants did not grow was that their seed was inherently deficient; the seed did not value life; the seeds' parents did not value growth, or the seed was lazy and did not try hard enough to grow. Imagine the assumptions my students would have made about how plants grow and develop if I had only used deficit theories to describe the process. The lack of understanding my students would have had about how environments shape the growth and development of the organisms that live in them would have lifelong consequences. Imagine it. Unfortunately for many poor and students of color, their teachers are the ones with the lack of understanding of how the environments that many students live in affect their growth and development. Instead of finding ways to help students who lack the resources and exposures recover those losses, they are instead blamed for circumstances that are out of their control. It's time to turn over a new leaf.

Conscious educators, however, are aware of the obstacles and hurdles their students face and seek to find ways to fill in any gaps in knowledge and skills missed due to this lack of exposure. Conscious educators find ways to empower their students not to succumb to their circumstances but to overcome them. When students enter the classroom lacking knowledge in mainstream ways of speaking, conscious educators don't admonish the home languages of those students and devalue them; instead, they help their students practice the art of "code-switching." They understand that students need to be able to keep their authentic sense of self while still being able to communicate when necessary with others more academically or universally (Gay, 2010). When students enter the classroom with cultural differences in interaction patterns, teachers don't assume their students are ill-mannered or out-of-control; instead, they model and practice the desired behaviors and customs necessary for a productive learning environment. Many teachers assume that what they believe are "good manners" are universal to everyone and fail to allow students the opportunity to adjust to their expectations, rules, and procedures. My heart aches every time I see a parent-bashing meme floating around, suggesting that if students only had "good manners," everything would be "easier" for teachers. Sure, there are many instances where students can be rude; that's human nature. However, students may not always be familiar with a particular teachers' idea of what good manners are. Therefore, teachers must model those expectations, patiently and consistently. Finally, when students enter the classroom with cultural knowledge outside of mainstream norms, conscious educators use their students' cultural strengths and knowledge to build on the new learning needed for academic success. However, teachers cannot do this work alone.

When students enter classrooms lacking exposure to the social capital that allows them to understand mainstream ways of speaking, acting, and knowing, educational researcher Stephen W. Raudenbush (2012) says that not only should there be changes in how teachers approach these students, but there are school policies needed that also reduce the impact of racial and social inequality as well. Such practices which include increasing the "amount, quality, and equity in schooling" have been proven to benefit students who enter the classroom with a lack of experiences in mainstream norms. These increases can include but are not limited to expanding early childhood learning opportunities through preschool initiatives, extending the school year to fend off the effects of summer slides, increasing the number of experienced teachers, and increasing teacher knowledge of subject areas. However, not included in this list is a practice that is not seen as an increase, but as a much-needed reduction. This reduction should come in the form of class-size. The many and most recent teacher walkouts and strikes echoing this demand is a strong indication that many teachers are already knowledgeable of the benefits of such practices (Romero, 2019). School administrators and policymakers should take heed to teacher concerns and demands in this matter.

Teachers who develop the skills to identify the needs of a child experiencing some degree of lack of opportunity do their best to help those students compensate for that loss. These teachers, the ones that can still see value, worth, intelligence, and talent in these students are going to be the ones who can help them make significant changes in their lives simply because they cared enough to try. These teachers are what Gloria Ladson-Billings (2009) refers to as the "dreamkeepers." These teachers realize that one doesn't have to reach perfection in order to help students in the classroom; they just realize that being compassionate and understanding towards students helps one get close enough.

The power of a culturally responsive teacher cannot be fully expressed in words. The positive impact and progress a teacher can make with a student when they become knowledgeable of who that student is individually and culturally is ten-fold. When teachers seek to increase their knowledge of the histories, perspectives, values, and beliefs of culturally, linguistically, and socioeconomically diverse students they are better able to create learning experiences that are more meaningful and relevant to their students' needs. Not only is having increased knowledge of students' cultural backgrounds helpful in increasing positive learning opportunities, but it is also essential to creating more positive relationships as well.

CHAPTER 4

THE CULTURALLY CARING CLASSROOM

T he power of culturally responsive teaching cannot be properly obtained without the inclusion of culturally responsive caring. This kind of caring is not based on typical superficial nods to being nice, saying kind words, or simple gestures of sympathy or empathy towards students. In a culturally responsive classroom, caring includes authentic and deliberate attention not only to students' academic well-being but their social and emotional well-being as well. A culturally caring teacher doesn't just say they care about all students; they engage in the actions necessary to prove it. These actions can most commonly be observed in teachers who have built authentic relationships with students, held high expectations for them, and value and affirm the cultures they come into the classroom with (Gay, 2010). Unfortunately, many teachers restrict their efforts in caring for students and only reserve even their most superficial attempts for those students they deem worthy and valuable enough to receive it. These other students, who are unfortunate enough to be viewed in ways that are intolerable, inappropriate, or otherwise problematic are at an increased disadvantage, as many teachers' ability to show care for students comes on a conditional basis. The effects of an aesthetically caring teacher as opposed to an authentically caring teacher cannot be summed up more clearly than in the story of a former student of mine named David.

David was a student whose reputation preceded him. He had transferred from a nearby pre-k, and his previous teacher had called ahead to warn his new teacher Mrs. Jones of who David was. After hearing from his former teacher about all the "trouble" the newest kindergartener had gotten into during his pre-k year, Mrs. Jones was worried. Not only was she worried, but she was also scared. She previously had a rough year with a group of second graders; she didn't know if she could handle the baggage that David was coming to school with.

About two weeks into school, David had already lived up to his reputation. Often, as the teachers typically gathered around to discuss the day, Mrs. Jones would sigh as she described the gamut of discipline behaviors she was dealing with while having David in her class. Her laments ranged from the run of the mill noncompliance to speaking out of turn and general "busyness." She would also often complain that he was breaking the materials in her centers, crying, and falling asleep in class. He wouldn't complete any assignments. She didn't know what to do. When she complained to me about his disruptive behaviors, I replied with the typical ancient remedies of loss of privileges, timeouts, or phone calls home (I was still developing in my critical consciousness at the time). She said she had tried that. She said nothing worked. She said he was ruining her lessons and she spent most of her time redirecting and trying to get him to stop crying during instruction. She also mentioned that she had to keep a close eye on him because he allegedly had "abused" another student in his pre-k class. Mrs. Jones had her hands full.

Another month passed, and Mrs. Jones became increasingly unable to manage David. One day after school, when she was once again lamenting about the problems with David, I stopped her and asked if I could see this "monster of a child" she had been complaining about for so long. My request was granted. Based on the stories she had told, I had imagined a scary little demon-child with snarling teeth, devil horns, and a pitchfork to match. I was curious as to what I would encounter. The next day, I walked into Mrs. Jones' class and asked her to point out David. To my surprise, I did not see a menacing, snarling, monster of a child. Instead, I saw a short, round, plump-faced, well-dressed, African American boy sitting on a large alphabet rug, happily eating his morning snack. "That's David?" I turned to her, surprised. "Yes!" she replied sharply. To me, he was the cutest little thing I had seen in a while and in kindergarten, that was not hard to come by. After seeing David, I decided to offer Mrs. Jones another solution to dealing with his behaviors. In my personal school experiences as a child and my professional teaching experiences, I already knew that sometimes White teachers had a hard time relating to Black children, particularly boys. This wasn't the first time I had to help a colleague with a seemingly uncontrollable little Black boy. Unfortunately, I was the only African American teacher for the grade level.

Energized with a new approach, I told her that if he gave her any more trouble to send him to me. As teachers, we often swapped kiddos that we needed a break from. I also wanted to see how David would respond in my classroom. It had also been my experience that many Black children behave differently in a classroom with a teacher of the same ethnic background. Research on this phenomenon in schools has revealed as much as well (Dee, 2004). It wasn't long before Mrs. Jones brought David into my classroom because he had been disruptive in hers. When he arrived, I welcomed David into my classroom and had him sit at a desk to complete the work he would not do while he was in Mrs. Jones' class. The results of this first interaction between David and I would set off a chain of events that would send me on a journey in becoming a genuinely conscious educator, even before I knew what a conscious educator was.

The first thing I noticed when David walked into my room was how sad he looked. He looked broken and ashamed. He was also mad and had dried tears stained on his face. When he sat down at the desk, I asked him to complete his work. He replied that he didn't know how. While my students were busy during their Writer's Workshop, I sat with David to complete his work. He didn't give me any problems and listened very well while we worked together. When we had completed the assignment from his teacher, I took the opportunity to speak with him about the behavior that brought him to me in the first place. I reminded him that I expected him to do his best and that he was a smart boy who shouldn't be getting into trouble. I told him that I didn't want him to have to come back to my classroom because he was misbehaving in his homeroom. He agreed and remained in my classroom a little while longer until his teacher came to retrieve him. I had hoped our little chat and visit would help David when he returned to his regular classroom. Unfortunately, David's behavior continued to escalate.

I continued to hear stories about his disruptions and his lack of compliance. As a result, he regularly came to my classroom when his behavior became too much for Mrs. Jones to handle. While in my classroom, we would complete his assigned work from his homeroom, and I would send him back to Mrs. Jones when he was done. Not long after, this routine had gotten old for all parties involved, and David's mother requested that he be moved to another classroom, permanently. When asked what classroom she would like her son to be moved to, she requested mine. I was informed of the transition by an administrator the day before it was to happen. I was, of course, nervous about taking on another student, but I didn't hesitate to accept him because I didn't want him to feel unwanted. I assured my administrator that he would get a clean slate when he arrived and that I would treat him just as I would any new student.

When David came to my classroom, I had a mission to make a positive impact on him because I genuinely cared about him, just as I cared about all of my students. I wanted him to experience a classroom where he was welcomed and accepted. To the surprise of many, David's behavior and academic achievements changed once he was introduced to a learning environment that was more culturally caring and responsive to his learning needs. When David entered my classroom, he didn't enter with the horror stories from his previous teacher. He entered as a new student. In his previous classroom, he had often been isolated from other students; I wanted him to feel a part of the classroom. In my classroom, he was no longer isolated from others; he was given a seat at a table with his classmates and a spot next to others at the carpet. When David displayed trouble following classroom rules, he was redirected and encouraged to do his best. When he attempted to fall asleep in class, he was made to stand up and stretch and get back to work. I also mentioned his tired demeanor to his mother and how important it was for David to be alert during instruction. She apologized and said that she often caught him getting up to watch T.V. in the middle of the night. She assured me the problem would be solved. It was; he no longer slept in my class.

When David seemed to be looking for negative attention, which he was accustomed to, he was not indulged. He was, however, enthusiastically praised when he got back on track. There was no permanent record of his wrongs; we addressed issues as they arose, and moved on. Every day was a clean slate. The transition to my classroom seemed to be what he needed in helping him become the student he had always wanted to be. Did David become the perfect student? No. Was I a perfect teacher? Absolutely not. The difference was that I was able to develop a caring and authentic relationship with David. He knew I cared; as a result, he aimed to please. In the making of this relationship with David, I used my knowledge of his individual and cultural strengths and interests to help keep him engaged in activities he previously struggled in. When I found out that he was a budding and talented drummer in his family church, I used it to my advantage. David, who once fidgeted and squirmed uncontrollably during carpet time, transformed into a focused musician as the official beat maker during songs and dances. He was brilliant! Now, not only did David participate more often in classroom activities, but he was also seen in a new light by his classmates. His confidence now soared. He even began to make some friends finally.

David would continue to improve while in his new classroom environment. He would show growth in demonstrating positive interactions with classmates. He would show growth in gaining academic skills and the completion of his own assignments. He happily participated during instruction. However, he still continued to endure negative interactions with other teachers. While I did my best to shield him from this, I was often reprimanded. I became isolated from my teammates as a result. I was told I was "treating him special" by other colleagues, and I could sense resentment from his former teacher begin to build between us. She also didn't hold back her feelings for David as he would often smile and say hello to her in the hallway, in which she often returned a glare in his direction. Even though I was making progress with him, my teammates and some of my administrators, unable to see his value, could also not see his growth and progress. They could not authentically care for David. They had not yet become culturally caring educators. If teachers are truly invested in making sure every student is cared for and treated in more loving ways, we must get to the bottom of what prevents many teachers from doing so.

Actions Speak Louder than Nice Words

Many teachers value general kindness and politeness as essential character traits to determine if someone is a "good teacher." Often times, these "good teachers" are praised for smiling, using feel-good language, never complaining, or using a soft tone. In the era of technology, one who "tweets" a lot about their classroom is also perceived in the same positive light. These are just a few of the many ways in which teachers assess one another's capacity to be "caring" in superficial ways. While these may be the true emotions of many teachers, they can also be superficial ways of portraying a caring attitude for the sake of job performance. If teachers are aiming to become more conscious of how to be a more culturally responsive and therefore culturally caring educator, please leave all the aesthetics of caring at the door, only authentic caring teachers are allowed any further.

Creating a classroom environment where all students feel welcomed, accepted, and cared for is a goal all teachers aim for and undoubtedly try to attain. If one would ask a teacher how they show how they care about their students, one is bound to get a range of answers that revolve around "treating everyone with respect," "treating everyone the same," or even the basic "I care about all my students." Unfortunately, when many poor and students of color are asked how their teachers feel about them, the answers are unnervingly opposite when they say that their teachers "don't care," or that they "don't like" them. If teachers are thinking that students who get on their nerves or who they "can't stand" have no clue because they "treat everyone the same," chances are they are not as good an actress (or actor) as they think. I thought I was once a good actress when I was having trouble with one of my Nigerian students, Samuel. I was so bad at it that once, after one of my annual classroom observations, my supervising principal called me out and said: "It looks as though you do not like him." She was right. I didn't, and it showed. Teachers invested in creating more caring environments for every student must begin to reflect on the barriers that get in the way. For teachers with students from diverse backgrounds in their classrooms, they must reflect on any negative racial biases, negative stereotypes, and otherwise ethnocentric attitudes within which can keep their capacity to care for diverse students at bay. For many teachers, this can be a painful and challenging process. Nonetheless, it is critically necessary to do so.

Recent research conducted by Rutgers professor Dan Batty concluded that White teachers were "three times more negative with Black students than with white students" (Rosario, 2019). He cited that many of the interactions between these students and their teachers were escalated when teachers reacted more negatively to student emotions and ability. I know this much to be true from my own experiences as a student, as a substitute teacher once mocked my mannerisms by "rolling" his neck and snapping his fingers at me. Then again, in college, when a professor attempted to humiliate me and hold me to a different standard when I was late to class. These experiences continued when another professor, stopped instruction to reprimand the face I was making while she was teaching. Unfortunately, the subjective manner in which I was disciplined because someone in authority did not like my "attitude" is representative of a disproportionate number of young Black girls and women alike. The misunderstanding that many non-black people have in regards to the "verve" and emotion present within the communication styles of many African Americans is often perceived as aggressive, angry, combative, or disrespectful (Gay, 2010). Batty concluded his research by recommending that teachers check their racial bias. Schools could also help overturn these negative experiences on behalf of their African American students by hiring more Black teachers. He concluded that Black teachers had more positive interactions with Black students. These results could be viewed as a case of cultural mismatch; it could also be a symptom of something a little harder to define.

"Microaggressions" is a term that has gained attention in the new culture of racial outing. Microaggressions are often described as the "indirect, subtle, or even unintentional ways that teachers discriminate against students of color and other marginalized student groups" (Baker, 2019). Typically, teachers who are unaware of the microaggressions they are projecting onto students often only view themselves as enforcing rules and procedures. Unfortunately, many teachers, in their attempts to control student behaviors, end up exacerbating them in their approach. Consequently, many of the rules teachers attempt to reinforce are not only unnecessary for ensuring the safety of the learning environment; they can also be viewed as racially motivated. When teachers micromanage behaviors such as hat wearing, correct use of standard English, or use of tone or body language, teachers need to reflect on why they feel the need to discipline such behaviors. Many times, cultural differences in values, beliefs, and displays of respect between teachers and students vary considerably between cultural groups. Teachers invested in creating caring and welcoming environments for every student should investigate why certain non-threatening student behaviors bother them to determine if it is something that is just a pet peeve, a cultural difference, or if it genuinely deserves disciplining. Unfortunately, microaggressions are not only complicit in creating uncaring environments for students of color; they are also complicit in creating them for teachers as well.

My last year of teaching kindergarten was one of the most difficult in terms of dealing with my colleagues. I had not been on campus long before I experienced mistreatment and contempt from my teammates and fellow teachers. Sure, I was met with smiles in the hallway and general salutations of "good morning" and "good afternoon" throughout the day. However, I was typically avoided in conversations. One teammate even perpetually changed her seating if she found herself to be sitting next to me. I was ignored during team planning discussions; however, my ideas were often regurgitated by someone else and suddenly deemed valuable. I was isolated from team gatherings and happenings, because, well, no one spoke to me if they didn't have to. This was frustrating. I was new to the campus, was the only Black teacher on the team, and I was getting the feeling that many of my new teammates were not comfortable being around Black people. I also felt it was particularly difficult for my colleagues to embrace me because I openly spoke about teaching in culturally responsive ways. Most of them were unfamiliar and resistant to the concept.

To avoid being assumptive, I decided to observe how my other new, White teammate was treated. I noticed a significant difference. She was included in every conversation, invited to team lunches, and even asked what kind of food she preferred to eat. None of which had ever happened between my new teammates and me. I was usually asked to join in on team lunches after everyone else had already decided where they were going to go, had grabbed their purses, and were on their way to their cars. My team leader would stick her head in my classroom on their way to the parking lot and ask me if I wanted to join them for lunch. I seemed just to be an afterthought.

My colleagues understood the aesthetics of caring. They had the smiles, early morning greetings, and nice words. What they lacked was *authenticity*. They didn't genuinely care about me because I was different from them, had different values than them; and therefore, was not valuable enough to be worth the effort to actually include or get to know. For my former teammates and many White teachers, the lack of authentic exposure to diverse people growing up can leave teachers ill-prepared to interact authentically with people of color. This is not ideal in an increasingly diverse and global society such as the U.S. It is even less ideal in increasingly diverse classrooms and schools.

Unlike myself, young and developing children may not be able to just "shake it off" when their teacher treats them in a less than exemplary manner. When students feel that their teachers do not care or are exhibiting conscious or unconscious racist beliefs or bias towards them, such implications can have devastating effects on student achievement. Michael D. Anderson's (2016) article highlights Northwestern University's research on the impact of racism on students. He notes that:

> *[T]he physiological response to race-based stressors — be it perceived racial prejudice, or the drive to outperform negative stereotypes — leads the body to pump out more stress hormones in adolescents from traditionally marginalized groups. The effects of these stressors lead to lower grades, less motivation, and less persistence during academic challenges.*

Teachers must counter these effects with more authentic and caring interactions with diverse students. Teachers must begin to create culturally caring classrooms and schools.

Just as I could tell my colleagues didn't like me, students also know when their teachers authentically care about them, too. Authentically caring teachers in the context of culturally relevant teaching are the backbone of its successful implementation. It shows itself through the positive "teacher attitudes, expectations, and behaviors about students' human value, intellectual capability, and performance responsibilities" (Gay, 2010, p. 48). Educational researcher and culturally responsive trailblazer Geneva Gay places "caring interpersonal relationships" as crucial in culturally responsive teaching. She characterizes it as "patience, persistence, facilitation, validation, and empowerment." By contrast, "uncaring ones are distinguished by impatience, intolerance, dictations, and control." (p. 49). The latter is more consistent with the school climate of many campuses.

To me, the clearest example of this kind of control in schools revolves around teachers' restrictions on bathroom breaks for students. As a novice teacher, I learned the ropes of what it meant to be a "good teacher" by copying what the other, more experienced teachers around me did. Among the behaviors I mimicked was the strict use of the restroom pass in the classroom. The rationalization that students who need to go to the bathroom more than once in a certain amount of time are "only playing" or "trying to get out of doing work" was told to me so many times, I began to believe it. Don't get me wrong; this can definitely be true for some instances. I too, have left meetings or workshops simply because I needed a break or was bored. Students who feel unengaged or have undiagnosed learning difficulties may also use the restroom as an escape during academic challenges. However, the risk of a student having an accident in their chair or on the carpet because they were too afraid to ask to go to the bathroom became too great a risk for me to take. I re-evaluated the restroom policy. Unfortunately, many colleagues never came to that conclusion and continued to scold students who had accidents because they denied access to the bathroom. The most extreme case of this happened when a teacher refused a young boy's request to use the restroom and instead decided he should use the trashcan in the front of the classroom (KCAL/ KCBS/ CNN, 2019). This incident is unacceptable, and teachers need to reflect on why they feel the need to control so badly when and how often students use the restroom. What harm will it do to allow a student to go as they please? Teachers must be able to reflect on these issues and more if we are ever going to reach the point where every student has the opportunity to have a caring classroom environment. Teachers must be the model in creating these caring environments. To do so, teachers must know what authentic caring looks like in order for students to also accurately mimic it themselves.

Replacing Punitive Discipline Practices

It is undeniable that schools should be a place where students can learn good morals and values to help them function in the real world. Many school-wide core values are themed around being a good citizen, remembering that kindness counts, and, more recently, to tolerate diversity. The fervor of many schools' anti-bullying stances has emerged out of these professed values. In turn, many schools' codes of conduct have increased the consequences of bullying and created a "zero tolerance" response to such behaviors.

However, the tragic and frequent occurrence of school shootings and suicide among youth across the country is an indication that just being nice may not be good enough. Schools are fraught with linguistically, ethnically, and religiously different people; therefore, the aims of schools should no longer be to teach students to be "nice" to people different than themselves; but understanding, inclusive, and affirming as well. In order to create more culturally aware students and teachers, schools need to understand the messages and values about diversity being sent and how to redefine them to be more culturally responsive and caring to the needs of all students.

Any review of the latest news headlines will reveal that many schools are still struggling to make the experiences of all students as equitable and "kind" as possible. From a young girl being flipped over in her desk by a police officer over a cell phone to the handcuffing of an autistic child in the midst of a meltdown, the traumatic stories of students who are culturally different being treated in inhumane and often cruel ways are too common for comfort (The Associated Press, 2016; Austrew, 2016; Guerrero, 2018). The continued presence of racial disparities in school discipline rates for students of color across America may not be sending the intended message to "treat others with kindness." According to a study reported by The Southern Poverty Law Center, students of color are suspended at rates five times greater than their White counterparts who commit the same offenses (Brownstein, 2015). The culprit is the presence of many teachers' implicit bias against students of color. Researchers at Yale also released the results of their study in regards to how teachers view students and their approach to discipline. Their researchers found that many teachers identified misbehaviors more often in Black students, even when there was no misbehavior apparent (Brown, 2016). These results are not uncommon as many teachers have expressed views that they believe students of color, particularly Black, are more aggressive, hostile, and disruptive than their White counterparts (Young, 2016). Teachers have got to make some changes.

Schools committed to students being kind and treating others with respect need to also look at how their teachers are treating their students. When educators are observed passing judgment, behaving in inappropriate and criminal ways, and then disciplining students that they feel are engaging in inappropriate, threatening, or otherwise unwelcomed behaviors, what message does that project? Schools can continue to say they care about all students, chant it, plaster it on the walls, and send it home in newsletters every week, but ultimately actions speak louder than words.

When teachers discipline students of color more harshly than their White counterparts for the same infractions, their actions say they are intolerant of their mistakes. The same message is conveyed when teachers call the campus police on students during a discipline infraction such as cell-phone use. When teachers discourage students of color from wearing culturally affirming hairstyles, they are saying their culture is not appropriate. When they seek to separate groups of children of color from socializing together, it projects the message that teachers are afraid of them. These instances are not sending the message that we love and care about our students; instead, these instances say, they must be controlled.

Schools that genuinely want to teach students to be good citizens and to treat others the way they want to be treated can look to the promises of restorative justice. According to the Center for Justice and Reconciliation, restorative justice is a disciplinary approach that seeks to repair the harm done by an offender and offers them a chance to reconcile the offense by working together with the offended to come up with solutions to solve the problem (Center for Justice and Reconciliation, 2018). Teacher and author Linea King discuss the benefits of this approach in her 2015 article entitled "Baby Steps Toward Restorative Justice." In her article, King discusses how she has used restorative justice approaches in her classroom and the benefits of doing so. Ultimately, instead of contributing to the school-to-prison pipeline by suspending and expelling students for misbehaviors, she kept them in class. Instead of disparaging students about their undesirable behavior, she reminded them of their worth and goodness. Instead of leaving the resolution in the hands of the offender, the class community worked together to formulate ways to interact differently in the future. In the end, she did not have perfect students, but she did have fewer classroom altercations, increased classroom community building, and students with living examples of how to work through their problems with others (King, 2015). Schools committed to ensuring the safety and well-being of all students should take a look at the messages they are sending when they are intolerant and often unforgiving of the common adolescent behaviors their students exhibit.

Different, Not Less

When self-professed caring teachers conduct themselves in uncaring ways, a closer look at deficit-mindset thinking can also shed light on the potential causes of these outcomes. The deficit thinking model says that "the student who fails in school does so because of his/her internal deficits or deficiencies. Such deficits manifest, adherents allege, in limited intellectual abilities, linguistic shortcomings, lack of motivation to learn, and immoral behavior" (Valencia, 2010, p. 6-7). These alleged deficits can play out in classrooms in several ways. Valencia (2010) details how these deficit theories manifest themselves in victim blaming, oppressing the victim, reliance on pseudoscience, inferior culture or temporal changes, the educability of students, and heterodoxy" (p. 18). Victim blaming is seen when teachers place the weight of school failure solely on the shoulders of the students and their parents that experience it. Students are further oppressed when those failures relegate them to lower tracked classes which place them further behind students in higher tracked or advanced placement courses. Although the most egregious acts of pseudoscience have been eliminated in the discourses of student failure, cultural deficit theories still abound. Many teachers still hold onto the notion that poor and students of color fail because of some defect in their upbringing, cultural practices, or language. This, in turn, leads many teachers to reduce their confidence in and lower their expectations of the abilities of such students. As a result, the insidiousness of deficit theories plays out in self-fulfilling prophecies for many marginalized students. Many teachers have not come to the conclusion that differences are not deficits.

One culprit in the continued deficient-oriented assumptions regarding students of color is the continued comparison of them to White cultural norms. The false sense of normalcy placed on Eurocentric, middle-class norms leads many teachers unable to see the cultural assets of their diverse students. The lack of ability to view diverse students through a strength-based lens continuously harms them as teachers often compare them to what they lack in whiteness. Many schools are still culturally unresponsive to the cultural ways of their ethnically diverse students and often view their lack of adherence to dominant cultural norms as deficits. This practice often lets the inequitable teaching practices and school policies off the hook, as teachers are more focused on "fixing" what is wrong with students instead of addressing the inequalities present in the classroom or school. Culturally caring teachers are less focused on fixing students and more concerned with making adjustments to the school culture and classroom climate, which continues to harm academic achievement.

In the case of my former student David, at least three of the deficit-oriented characteristics mentioned above were projected onto him by teachers in the school. The presence of these factors played significant roles in his ability to succeed in school. Oppressive forces were often used against him by other teachers, with the most egregious instance happening in the cafeteria. One morning, he was denied the opportunity to eat breakfast by another teacher because he "wouldn't stand in line properly." When he walked into my classroom crying because of what had happened, I escorted him to the cafeteria myself and helped him purchase his food. I let him eat it in my classroom. I rationalized that denying him the opportunity to eat would not have taught him a lesson on how to stand in line; instead, it would have only hurt his entire day and affected his ability to focus because he would only be able to think about how hungry he was. Denying students access to their basic human needs is not good discipline. It's cruel and unusual punishment. His educability was also threatened as the intellectual potential of David was doubted as his former teacher asserted minimal effort in trying to even keep him awake in class. If teachers want to rid schools of experiences such as this, teachers must begin to shift their mindsets regarding the abilities of their students. Teachers cannot expect students to overcome the obstacles stacked against them and attempt in even the smallest way that they are willing and able to be more if educators can't even bring themselves to visualize it as well.

Caring in Action

When teachers do not have "positive attitudes toward, expectations of, and interactions with students of color" it can cause them to "devalue, demean, and even fear" their ethnically, religiously, and linguistically diverse students (Gay, 2010, p. 48). In recalling the student David, it was clear there was very little opportunity for David to be successful in Mrs. Jones' class. From the moment his previous teacher called to "warn" her about David's behaviors, his chances of success decreased. From the moment Mrs. Jones then proceeds to warn everyone else about him, he was set up for failure. David had no chance of succeeding in Mrs. Jones' class because she didn't expect him to. These low expectations that often accompany these negative attitudes can have disastrous effects on student achievement (Gay, 2010). Teachers have to be cognizant of the connection between the two. Banks (2019) reminds us that "student behavior and *teacher expectations* are related interactively. The more teachers expect from students academically, the more they are likely to achieve; the more academically successful students are, the higher teacher expectations are likely to be for them" (p. 146). The same is true for low expectations. The potential benefits for poor and students of color when teachers are conscious of and invested in more authentic ways of caring and connecting with their diverse students are endless and bountiful. Schools have yet to see the possibilities of what could happen when all students are in "environments where they feel comfortable and valued" (Gay, 2010, p. 232). I look forward to those future possibilities.

So how can teachers ensure that their classrooms are more culturally caring and responsive to their diverse student's needs? Geneva Gay (2010) explains this goal as a "functional profile of culturally responsive caring." This can include, but is not limited to providing a space where students feel respected and valued, being an academic and social confidant, acquiring knowledge of your culturally diverse students, helping students develop a critical consciousness, building confidence and compassion among students, acknowledging social, cultural, ethnic, racial, linguistic, and individual difference while refraining from prejudices, and provide academically and socially challenging experiences for all students (p. 52). Many of these practices could start before the school year even begins.

Instead of a traditional "Meet the Teacher" event, teachers can put into practice the professed "students first" moto and get to know their students and their families, first. To do this, swap out "Meet the Teacher" night with a "Meet the Student" or "Meet the Family" night. Instead of bombarding parents with a stack full of rules for their students to comply with, try meeting them. Make it casual, provide a little snack, and drink and talk with families in order to get to know *them*. Ask future students who they are, where their interests lie, and what they love to learn about. Take notes!

Teachers will be getting valuable information about student interests and motivations for learning. If one must hand out paperwork at this time, make it useful for interactions with future students and their families. A short family questionnaire (in multiple languages) will do.

Take this opportunity to ask families:

- What are their educational goals for their children?

- What values, traditions, and customs are relevant to their family?

- What past educational hurdles have their children overcome?

- What future mountains do they anticipate their student climbing?

- What is the best way to communicate with them? In what language? What time?

- What positive and negative experiences have their children had in school?

- What do they want to tell about the talents and strengths of their child?

Questions like these, among many others, can help illuminate what is important to students and their families from the beginning. In doing so, the tendency to rely on deficit thinking patterns when students struggle or need more help can be eliminated. When teachers learn about parents' work schedules and family dynamics, they are less likely to make assumptions or draw incorrect conclusions about parent involvement. Teachers will no longer jump to the conclusion that a child's parents do not care about their students' education because they don't answer phone calls. Armed with this valuable information, when a student struggles with math, teachers will know that math is not their favorite subject and they may need to pull in some of their interests to help make it relevant. Now when teachers can't reach a parent for a conference, they will know that they work two jobs and it is difficult for them to get time off of work. When a student is late to school from time to time, teachers know it is because they are in charge of getting their brothers and sisters off to school first because their single mother/father has to work. If teachers know who their students are, where they come from, and what they are dealing with, teachers may be more inclined to help them overcome the obstacles in their lives, not punish them for it. When teachers rethink what caring looks like in the classroom, and move towards more authentic ways of expressing it, teachers can begin to see those tangible results of more authentic relationships, increased and higher expectations, and the valuing and affirming the cultures students come into the classroom with.

Where is the Love?

Affording a student their personhood should not be determined by a hairstyle, an outfit, the presence of a tattoo, good behavior, or an "attitude." Nor should it be determined by any other superficial constraint meant to deny them fair treatment in an attempt to justify their mistreatment. Yes, schools are often competing with street life, YouTube, and the like for students' attention. However, if schools want to deter students from being attracted to these forces, they must begin to give students what they need: acceptance, love, and understanding. School is the one place where receiving these essential human dignities should not be restricted because teachers are unwilling to give it to those they feel don't deserve it. Love should be in abundance, even when students behave in unlovable ways. Acceptance should be extended, even if students carry themselves differently than teachers expect. All students should be extended an ear of understanding, even when teachers find it hard to relate to their realities. Every student deserves culturally caring and conscious educators; every student, every day, no exceptions.

Stories like David's are all too common in many schools across America. Because of this, it is imperative that teachers demonstrate authentic care towards their students and embody the characteristics which result in actions that ensure the most positive and equitable learning environments for every student. Through my experiences with David as a student, I gained an invaluable understanding of how teacher expectations influence student success (Gay, 2010). Having David in my class, I would see how students of color (particularly Black boys) were subject to harsher and more frequent disciplinary consequences than their White counterparts who commit the same offenses (Brownstein, 2015). I would see the deficit thinking many teachers harbor in regards to their students of color and their parents (Valencia, 2010). The cruelty some educators could exhibit to "teach kids a lesson" when they misbehave is undeniable. However, despite these observations, I would understand how having high expectations for all students can transform negative behaviors. The importance of relationships would become apparent as getting to know students as individuals would help to make deeper connections with them. Focusing on students' strengths and interests more than their flaws would help build their self-esteem and motivate them to do better. Withholding judgments against parents would help to build trust and cooperation with them to help their child succeed. Most of all, I would see what many educators have not realized yet; that many educators still have very far to go in understanding how to achieve higher levels of student success for all students. Becoming conscious educators means teachers must continue to work to improve equity and equality for all students in the classroom. However, opportunities for improvement cannot just come through in a commitment to caring about students, but also in caring about what is taught to students as well.

CHAPTER 5

CREATING CULTURALLY RELEVANT CURRICULUMS

"Education either functions as an instrument which is used to facilitate the younger generation into the logic of the present system and bring about conformity or it becomes the practice of freedom, the means by which men and women deal critically and creatively with reality and discover how to participate in the transformation of their world."

–Paulo Freire, *Pedagogy of the Oppressed*

E very teacher, at some point in their career, should stop and reflect on one fundamental question: Why teach? On the journey to becoming a more conscious educator, teachers not only need to examine their motives and purposes for teaching but also examine what they teach and how they teach it. Once teachers reflect on these essential questions, they also have to be able to answer what their preferred methods mean in their increasingly linguistically and ethnically diverse schools. Specifically, teachers must ask themselves if their chosen methods have been a hindrance or a help in creating equitable learning experiences for every one of their diverse students.

To Tell the Truth

The most significant aspect of a schools' commitment to equity is not only revealed in the amount of care extended towards students, but also in the curriculum they teach. Content speaks volumes to students about what kinds of knowledge are worth knowing and, most importantly, *whose* knowledge is worth knowing. While teaching at my last job, I was painfully reminded of how little the histories and experiences of ethnically and linguistically diverse peoples are valued in many public schools. Educators must be conscious of not only valuing mainstream knowledge, but the value of including the histories, perspectives, and experiences of diverse students as well. To do this, teachers must not only be committed to the presence of truth in their teaching methods but their content as well.

During a school-wide First Responders celebration, I was confronted with the intolerance of truth that permeated throughout the campus. Presented as a celebration in honor of the anniversary of September 11th, my fellow kindergarten teachers were "uncomfortable" bringing up the topic of 9/11 in the kindergarten classroom. This apprehension perplexed me, so I asked a simple question: *"How are we to celebrate our First Responders if we are not willing to teach students why we are celebrating them in the first place?"* The unfortunate responses I received ranged from "It makes me too sad to talk about it" to "It happened before they were born, so why do they need to know about it?" At that point, I concluded there was not adequate time to address the misinformed assumptions and negative attitudes of my teammates on this topic, so I planned to move forward and conduct my lesson as I deemed appropriate for my students.

My lesson's message was to explain the story of 9/11 in a way that was easy and appropriate for a kindergarten class. This included an explanation of why First Responders were so important on that day. I wanted my students to understand the truth, while also tapping into the spirit of 9/11 by conveying the message to them that no matter where they come from, they are all Americans. I chose the masterfully crafted children's book, *We Came to America* by Caldecott-Honor winning author, Faith Ringgold. This book retells the origin stories of the diverse peoples and cultures that came to America; it is a blending of an experience that connects Americans through the truth about immigration. On one of the pages in the book, it describes how African Americans arrived in this country, even addressing the uncomfortable truth about slavery. During this reading, one very inquisitive little girl raised her hand and asked why the people in the illustration had chains on them. I explained to her that African Americans were enslaved when they were brought against their will long ago. I told her that slavery was abolished, and this answer seemed to quell her inquiry. Teachers, if teaching about slavery is viewed as too sad, gruesome, or inappropriate a topic for primary students to tackle, think about the violence, profanity, and sexual innuendos they are exposed to in the form of video games, superhero movies, and music in the car on the way to school. I often have had conversations with students about why one shouldn't tell people that they are going to "blow them up," "cut their heads off," or use profane language in my kindergarten classrooms. In the midst of all the fantasy and violence to which many students are exposed, a little fact and historical truth will not cause any further harm.

While many of the gruesome details and stories about slavery are inappropriate to share at such a young age, introducing children to the truth about history and culture is invaluable to their understanding of the world at large, particularly when attempting to understand diverse peoples. Unfortunately, when that inquisitive little girl went home and expressed to her family all she had learned in the book, a complaint was made to my principal. Unfortunately, my principal and the girls' parents were not interested in understanding how a multiple perspectives approach to history helps even the youngest learner understand how past historical events help students make sense of the world today. I was told that I should "teach the standards."

I was reminded yet again of the practice of exclusion of diverse histories on this campus when I was asked to help facilitate my schools' annual Black History luncheon for my colleagues. I decided to provide the "history" portion of the event. I decided that instead of making the traditional list of African American firsts that usually passed as the extent of knowledge of Black history, I would create a timeline. This timeline would give a deeper understanding of the actual history of African Americans that would illuminate and connect historical events to the present state of Black America today. It was a brief, but inclusive telling of African American history from the pre-slavery kingdoms of Mali and Timbuktu to the aftermath of the European slave trade to the Civil Rights movement and even more recently Black Lives Matter movements. I was excited to have the opportunity to present African American history to help teachers get a deeper understanding of the culture and experiences of their African American students.

When it was time to run the slideshow that would loop throughout the luncheon, I set up the computer, turned on the accompanied music and went to teach my class. An hour had passed when I received an email from one of my administrators telling me they were unable to show my presentation in its entirety. They said they had to delete many slides that they felt were "divisive and controversial" and not in keeping with the "celebratory" theme of past luncheons. I was confused. Was this not for educators? Were teachers not responsible for teaching Black History in the curriculum? Were there not African American students and teachers on campus whose histories were just as crucial as the White history that was already included at length in the state curriculum? Apparently not. This incident was disappointing in that during the school version of a Black history "celebration," actual Black experiences and perspectives were not tolerated. I later expressed to my principal disappoint in the lack of understanding in the value of teachers having a deeper understanding of the histories and perspectives of the African American students in their charge. I was told that my slides were not appropriate for an elementary school. I was told that it was not my "job" to expose teachers to that kind of information. I had no idea that it was not my job to teach. I was unaware that even if one teaches elementary students, they are only supposed to have an elementary understanding of the histories that they are to teach them. As conscious educators, teachers cannot shy away from hard history; they cannot let feelings of discomfort get in the way of teaching students facts about history and events. As mentioned in chapter three, teachers need more than just surface knowledge of the cultures of their diverse students. Foods and festivals do not help teachers better understand their students, and it also does not help students understand themselves nor others.

Unfortunately, incidents like these are all too common on many public school campuses. The censoring, minimizing, whitewashing, and omitting of the complex histories of diverse students speaks volumes about what knowledge is valuable and, ultimately, *who* is valuable. This practice is the leading cause of the disinterest and disengagement many students of color exhibit throughout their school experiences (Gay, 2010). The racial achievement gaps that remain across the nation are not an indication that students have failed, but that schools have failed them. Unfortunately, the comfort of White teachers, administrators, parents, and students continues to water down or exclude the rich histories of culturally diverse students in curriculums. As a result, many educators and adults, in general, grow up with disillusioned perceptions of American history. Many are missing those critical understandings of historical events of the past and its effects on different groups of people to this day. In turn, many have been unable to make sense of today's tumultuous racial climate, the continued racial disparities in lack of quality education, healthcare, employment, and housing for many diverse groups. Many rely on victim-blaming and denial-based rationalizations. Many more are simply stuck in a state of perpetual historical confusion. The grand narratives of American exceptionalism, equity, and justice for all pushed unquestioningly and uncritically upon us in school have yet to release their grip. Many of the people still entangled in its snares are educators. Filling in those gaps and increasing teachers' understanding of the world at large, the practice of historical omissions and distortions of the histories and experiences of African, Latinx, Asian, and Native American people need to be resolved.

Whose History is it Anyway?

To begin including the knowledge of the histories of linguistically and ethnically diverse peoples, teachers must reflect on where to get more accurate and complete information on these topics. If teachers were thinking of relying on their corporate produced textbook, please reconsider. Unfortunately, if schools want to begin to teach more accurate and complete history to students, they must have more accurate sources to choose from. Sadly, many textbooks have been missing the mark. James Loewen's groundbreaking account of the failure of teachers to correctly teach diverse histories is brilliantly illuminated in *Lies My Teacher Told Me* (2007). In his work, Loewen highlights the lack of breadth and depth given to the histories and perspectives of people of color in the United States in everyday textbooks. He highlights common myths perpetuated in the retelling of Columbus' "discovery" in the Caribbean. He overturns the romanticized accounts of the adventures of the Founding Fathers; and illuminates many of the trumped-up stories alluding to the values of equality, liberty and justice for all. He underlines the common teaching practice of recounting these stories without making a clear connection to the enslavement, land stealing, and discriminatory policies needed to gain these liberties for the few.

Loewen's book is a much-needed wake-up call for truth and clarity in classroom practices. However, teachers cannot begin to correct these destructive practices until they come to terms with how these distortions of truth affect the lives of students.

Too many schools are stuck in an endless stream of Eurocentric norms and values with no consideration for how such a focus often harms diverse students. Even though school is one of the first places that students learn the necessary knowledge and skills for academic purposes, it is also the first place they are introduced and reinforced with mainstream norms of the dominant culture, i.e., White, middle-class, America. Many of the mainstream ideological notions of meritocracy, capitalism, and individualism are seeping from the pages of teachers' curriculum guides and manuals. The messages that schools promote about the idea of meritocracy and "hard work" as all it takes to succeed are inaccurate. The notion that everyone is an individual and no one is grouped in any shape by race, class, gender, ableness, religion, or sexual orientation, is dangerous for marginalized students who know these "ideas" to be untrue. From the moment students walk through the doors of their classrooms in kindergarten, they enter into a social system built for whiteness where they must deny themselves and their experiences and exchange them for the mythologies of White, middle-class, able-bodied, cis-gender norms, and all its many confinements.

Teachers must begin to think about the messages being sent to students of color when they are reinforcing these mythologies. Teachers must acknowledge the messages being sent to students of color when they are asked to celebrate holidays, wars, and state officials that ultimately represent the enslavement, genocide, or disenfranchisement of their people. Reflecting on the appropriateness of having Native American students celebrate Thanksgiving with turkey crafts and pumpkin pie recipes, which also represents a day of mourning for many of their people should be reconsidered. The appropriateness of making African American students participate in Fourth of July celebrations of freedom and liberty when their people were enslaved and not granted the same rights as others at that time should be re-evaluated. Teachers must reflect on the one-size-fits-all attitude of what patriotism looks like in American society and reconsider how the history of oppression and discrimination has placed many groups of color on the losing end of liberty and justice to this day. Teachers have to start thinking of more inclusive ways of incorporating the many perspectives and histories of diverse students. They must rethink teaching practices that leave only some with feel-good nods of patriotism and pride while leaving others yearning for a more authentic representation of themselves, their perspectives, and their histories. Unfortunately, history subjects are not the only classes that suffer from inaccurate misinformation. Math, science, writing, and literature classes have all been reduced to narrow, one-sided, monolithic, representations of people of color all in the name of uniformity. Educators on the path to consciousness and cultural responsiveness need tools to interrupt the harmful effects of this kind of teaching.

Moving Forward

Shifting from archaic, monolithic, and modernist approaches to teaching are going to require a multifaceted and critical approach. These practices, which stem from centuries of one-sided approaches, will not change overnight. There will be significant resistance. However, awareness will be a crucial first step. One cannot expect to change a curriculum they see nothing worth improving. If the above breakdown of the current failings in teaching accurate and complete history doesn't hit the spot for teachers, Carter G. Woodson's *The Mis-Education of the Negro*; Howard Zinn's *A People's History of the United States*; or Ronald Takaki's *A Different Mirror* can all help teachers assess what they thought was good history instruction and point towards the direction of a more accurate one. When reading these texts, teachers should reflect on the gaps present in their understanding of the nation's history and consider how they affect their ability to make connections for students. Teachers should reflect on the practice of teaching by way of memorization and regurgitation and the harm it inflicts on students' ability to think critically about historical pasts. Once awareness has been made, teachers must also adopt a more critical approach to their instructional practices and seek to reduce current historical biases with the inclusion of more culturally relevant curriculum and instruction. This integration of a more culturally diverse curriculum encompasses a variety of histories and experiences that relate to diverse students. According to Gay (2010), it is crucial to keep in mind that the purpose of incorporating a more culturally relevant curriculum is to "empower ethnically diverse students through academic success, cultural affirmation, and personal efficacy" (p. 127). Teachers should resist the urge to bombard students with simple Jeopardy-style trivia facts about diverse people. James A. Banks (2019) encourages teachers to increase students' exposure to a more critical understanding of content through his four-stage process of transforming the curriculum. He encourages teachers to move from the current practice of regurgitation of facts to a more critical, social justice, and action-oriented approach. He advocates teachers continue developing their curriculum by moving it from simple contributions or additive approaches to diversity to a more in-depth transformative approach of social action outcomes in the curriculum (p. 64). The ultimate goal is to create a more accurate, complete, and reflective curriculum for diverse students. To do this efficiently, teachers must first be able to reduce Eurocentric bias in the curriculum; they must also be able to analyze the textbooks for accuracy and completeness. Adding multiple perspectives and using critical questioning can help reduce bias in the curriculum and make room for more diverse narratives and experiences.

Once teachers have determined the quality of the content, they must begin to incorporate more culturally relevant teaching practices. Thankfully, there are numerous educational scholars who have approached this task in a variety of ways. Although there is not just one right way to present the curriculum in a more culturally responsive way, there are some key points to keep in mind. After all, the ultimate goal in trying to engage previously underachieving students is to design curriculum in ways that are more meaningful, relevant, and more representative of the experiences, perspectives, values, and communities from which students emerge. In short, teachers need to understand how to "tap into students' prior knowledge in ways that will pique their interest in learning, increase their levels of engagement, and encourage them to feel part of the learning process" (T.C. Howard, p. 76, 2010). Teachers, please heed the following suggestions below.

Two helpful guides in transforming the current Eurocentric curriculum can be found in *Beyond Heroes and Holidays* (2008) and *Anti-Bias Curriculum: Tools for Empowering Young Children* (1989). Both books are phenomenal in underscoring the importance of transforming curriculum with the integration of the histories, perspectives, and contributions of people of color, women, religiously diverse, low-income, homeless, differently abled, poor, migrant, and LGBTQ peoples. With the inclusion of these two resources, every student will get to see themselves represented in their learning experiences. It is important to note that in transforming curriculum, teachers are not to take the typical "tourist" approach to incorporate these different perspectives (Derman-Sparks, 1989). Teachers do not want to project a feeling of "otherness" when discussing the histories and contributions of marginalized groups. Activities such as multicultural festivals, holiday celebrations focusing on food and clothing should be avoided as the sole means of inclusion. These practices in isolation not only tokenize and trivialize marginalized groups, but they also do not reflect the daily lives and struggles of these groups. Teachers should no longer aim to focus on diverse peoples through the narrow lens of a special occasion. Teachers should seek more nuanced, accurate, complete, and inclusive representations of the diverse students in their class throughout the year.

Below are essential components to ensuring the curriculum is more culturally responsive to linguistically and ethnically diverse students. In general, teachers should aim to have a curriculum that consists of content that is:

- Meaningful to the diverse students in the classroom.

- Creates a strong sense of self-efficacy.

- Relevant to their lived experiences.

- Inclusive of their histories, cultures, perspectives, and contributions.

- Understanding of the current issues they face in their communities.

- Involves critical thinking and opportunities to analyze information from a variety of sources outside the textbook.

- Conscious of issues of injustice and empower students to critique events (historical and current).

- Helpful in students acquiring real-life decision-making and social justice minded skills.

(T.C. Howard, 2010, p. 76; Gay, 2010, p. 128; Banks, 2019, p. 94)

Making the content more meaningful to linguistically and ethnically diverse students has to begin with getting to know what is meaningful to students. In a perfect world, teachers would have a specific time throughout the school year to sit and chat with students about their daily goings-on. Unfortunately, teachers don't live in a perfect world and days are cramped with assemblies, state tests, benchmarks, in-service meetings, fire drills, and now intruder (shooter) drills. Educators just don't have the time. Thankfully, many teachers have used journal writing to remedy this problem. In allowing students to journal about their daily lives in their own words and on their own topics, teachers can get a keen insight into the inner workings of what matters to their students. Please note that these journal entries should not be used to pull out giant red pens and correct students' writing. I know it can be hard, but please resist the urge. Instead, use these journals to inform instruction and incorporate the likes, interests, and knowledge of students into their new learning.

Creating a strong sense of self-efficacy in students can be done in a myriad of ways. The growth mindset approach by Carol Dweck (2006) is an excellent start in helping students not only set learning goals, but it also provides an opportunity to give them positive language to help them overcome tough learning situations and develop perseverance. Building confidence in students is critical in the process of acquiring new and unfamiliar information and skills. Often teachers focus too much on giving the "right answer" and do not congratulate the initial effort. Teachers need to take advantage of students' mistakes and build on them as an opportunity to investigate what they are missing and how to encourage them to continue to work to accomplish goals. Mistakes are only proof that one is trying! Teachers should be in the habit of encouraging students to try and try again!

Making the content relevant to their lived experiences can be made difficult if teachers rely too heavily on assumptions and never find out what experiences their students have had. The all too common back-to-school writing assignment about "Where I went on summer vacation" can be a pitfall in a classroom full of children who do not have the opportunity to actually go on a vacation. Such is also the case for pre-determined writing prompts about what they would do in the snow, or other regional happenings need to be met with caution. Instead, utilize those moments when they have shared stories about their lives, interests, and hobbies, to help make connections to the new learning teachers are hoping to impart.

Making content inclusive of their histories, cultures, perspectives, and contributions can also be done through including critical questions whenever teachers are introducing new topics. Questions that ask whose voice is missing, whose point of view is expressed, and who was affected by historical events can turn any one-sided story, reference, or book into an opportunity to think critically, research for more information, and analyze from multiple perspectives any subject. For example, many schools discuss the contributions of Christopher Columbus in their curriculum. For conscious educators, this is the perfect time to apply critical thinking to the often incomplete and inaccurate portrayal of Columbus' voyages. Instead of the typical fantasized story of the *Niñã*, *Pinta*, and *Santa Maria*, ask critical questions. Questions like: If Columbus arrived on an island already inhabited by people, why do people always say he discovered it? How did the conquering of and forced slavery of the Arawak people affect their way of life? Why do some people celebrate Columbus although he enslaved, killed, and decimated another group of people? If one chooses to celebrate Columbus, what does that say about what they value? What does Columbus Day mean for the descendants of the Indigenous groups he conquered? A high point to bring up would be the debate to swap out Columbus Day with Indigenous People's Day to remember the lives that were lost and the people who were affected by Columbus' inquisitions. Bill Bigelow and Bob Peterson (1998) have an excellent teacher resource in *Rethinking Columbus: The Next 500 Years* to help teachers break down this process. Whatever method teachers choose, the goal is helping every student develop and maintain a positive racial identity and value for others' differences by including diverse histories and perspectives.

Incorporating critical thinking and opportunities to analyze information from a variety of sources outside the textbook can be done when teachers use primary sources, direct quotes, newspaper clippings, documentaries, and other reference materials to discuss events. Solely using textbooks can leave students without the ability to question the often-unquestionable tones used throughout many textbooks (Loewen, 2007). Instead of just reading in textbooks that Thomas Jefferson was a great president, find the evidence of it. Reading excerpts from his *Notes on the State of Virginia* (1785) and other publications will paint a very different and contradictory picture of this founding father. Discuss it! National heroes do not need to be presented in perfect holiness, but must be seen in their entirety to get an accurate picture of them. Again, continuing to push Eurocentric norms and values onto diverse students distorts the historical reality of America's history of colonialism and its effects on those groups colonized. Teachers should no longer aim to teach students what to think about American history, but how to think about it in more critical ways.

Gaining an understanding of the current issues students face in their communities would mean providing students opportunities to discuss the issues they face in their lives regularly. Morning meetings, community circles, or any opportunity for students to safely and without judgment, express the happenings in their lives is essential. This simple 5 to 10-minute morning or afternoon routine can also help raise consciousness about issues of injustice, and it can empower students to critique events while acquiring real-life decision-making and social justice-minded skills. When students bring up the issues they see in their communities, take the time to help them formulate solutions. Incorporate them into the regular curriculum. Persuasive writing assignments are perfect activities to strengthen practical writing skills and incorporate research and debate. Teachers may be surprised to see how compassionate, caring, and introspective many students can be when they are allowed to discuss issues that are relevant to their lives.

Taking the time to rethink current teaching practices is critical in improving the learning opportunities of marginalized students. Developing a more meaningful and relevant curriculum will open up the possibilities of seeing all that students are capable of doing. Conscious educators are aware of how critical a more relevant curriculum is to the academic success of their students. Conscious educators seek, every day, to ensure more equitable learning opportunities that bring every student one step closer to actualized academic success.

What About the White Kids?

With so much emphasis placed on inclusion, one may question what all of this means for White students. Thankfully, no study shows any harm has ever come to White students from being exposed to more accurate and complete representations of those ethnically, linguistically, or religiously different from themselves (Logan & Oakley, 2012). Being exposed to different viewpoints, perspectives, and people only help students learn to appreciate, accept, and positively interact with those different than themselves. Numerous educators and scholars can attest to the improved sense of self, and positive understandings of others, that many White teachers and students experience when they are exposed to the many narratives that make up American history (Howard, 2016). Imagine the difference in political commentaries and public policies if the majority of White people who currently hold negative and deficit attitudes about diverse peoples had experienced a culturally responsive curriculum during their K-12 education. Yes, many detractors of more culturally responsive education will try to simplify its purposes to "feel good" notions only meant for students of color. However, this is not true. Culturally responsive teaching is for ALL students. No one will be left out. Not only will there be a change in student performance, but they will also "develop more positive intergroup attitudes and values" (Banks, 2019, p. 57). Isn't that what schools want for 21st-century students to know how to do? Again any look at the continuous stream of headlines of blackface on college campuses, confrontations with Indigenous elders and the like, are a clear indication that more culturally responsive approaches to instruction will not only help students of color be included, mainstream students will learn the importance of how to include and value those different from themselves as well (Keneally, 2019; Ross, 2016).

Culturally Responsive Teaching is Effective Teaching

The advantages of incorporating more culturally responsive practices in teaching have been noted in numerous longitudinal studies and programs over time and have given anecdotal and empirical evidence to its success when implemented correctly (Smith, 1998). Culturally responsive programs such as the Algebra Project, which integrated community instruction with math; Funds of Knowledge, which used home and school to make connections to learning; the Puente Project, which is a community mentor program for high school and college students; the Harlem Children's Zone, and the Lemon Grove Academy, have all noted success (Pang, 2018).

Programs that are no longer implemented, such as the Javits Project, which found success in providing increased exposure to marginalized students in Gifted and Talented programs, can also be looked at for inspiration in the effectiveness of culturally responsive practices. They noted significant changes in not only student success in higher-level courses, but the transformative power of changing deficit-minded teachers into culturally affirming ones once teachers exposed students to more challenging curriculum (Swanson, 2016). Culturally responsive teaching has the power to change the current underperforming outcomes of marginalized students and bring about the positive changes of embracing cultural assets, more caring learning environments, more relevant curriculum, challenging racial stereotypes, and allowing schools to become change agents for social justice in continuing struggles for equality (Gay, 2010).

Teachers dedicated to providing more effective teaching for their diverse students can go about implementing this transformative teaching process in more than one way. Many scholars have categorized successful methods to use in implementing culturally responsive practices from Geneva Gay, Zaretta Hammond, Christine Sleeter, and Sonia Nieto, to name a few. All, which can be used as excellent references for culturally responsive practices. James A. Banks (2019) has revolutionized the components of culturally responsive teaching through his development of the multicultural education framework. Multicultural education along with culturally responsive teaching both "incorporates the idea that all students — regardless of their gender, sexual orientation, social class, and ethnic, racial, linguistic, or cultural characteristics — should have an equal opportunity to learn in school" (p.1). In many aspects, both approaches are one in the same. Both approaches seek to include the cultural frames of reference of students. Both approaches engage students to think critically about the information they receive. Together they seek to create the most inclusive learning environments by addressing and reducing prejudice, and both seek to challenge the current educational status quo by making sure that certain policies and practices are student-centered and not teacher-dominated. His five dimensions of multicultural education can be used to help teachers gather more tools and methods for incorporating more culturally responsive teaching practices.

The Framework

Banks (2019) breaks down the practices to ensure the most effective instruction for culturally and linguistically diverse students into five critical components: content integration, the knowledge construction process, prejudice reduction, equity pedagogy, and empowering school culture and social structure (p. 43). Teachers can use the dimensions as a guideline to ensure the most authentic application of culturally responsive teaching practices.

Content integration refers to "the extent to which teachers use examples, data, and information from a variety of cultures and groups to illustrate the key concepts, principles, generalizations, and theories in their subject area or discipline" (Banks, 2019, p. 45). Typically, many educators assume this piece is the only aspect of culturally responsive teaching. Within this assumption, content integration can be seen as a side note or special occasion inclusion during a holiday. As discussed earlier, this is not culturally relevant. When students only see relevant reflections of their histories and cultures on occasions, it can send the message of "otherness" regarding diverse students' cultures and heritages. It can give the unintended message that the constant Eurocentric inclusions of history, perspectives, and holidays are the "real" curriculum and everything else is just extra. This misunderstanding of this element of curriculum ultimately fuels the often-cited grievance of some when they lament that there is no "White History Month." There is no need, as White history, culture, and norms are overly abundant in many school experiences. However, effective culturally responsive teachers understand that every student matters every day, and they seek to include diverse frames of reference, cultural icons, heroes, issues, and perspectives *throughout* the year.

The knowledge construction process "describes the procedures by which social, behavioral, and natural scientists create knowledge and how the implicit cultural assumptions, frames of reference, perspectives, and biases within a discipline influence the ways that knowledge is constructed within it" (Banks, 2019, p. 45). Central to the successful implementation of this component is the understanding of how learning is influenced by the cultural influences of the knower. Differences in culture, ethnicity, language, gender, sexual orientation, socioeconomic status, ability, and religion all influence the way knowledge is interpreted. Culturally responsive teachers need to be able to help students understand how to question knowledge presented to them by taking a multiple perspectives approach to their teaching. Providing students with more than one way of looking at issues, events, and problems from various points of view can help give them a more well-rounded take on events and develop their critical thinking skills. When teachers provide multiple perspectives on historical events such as the framing of the Declaration of Independence, the story of Thanksgiving, and even Columbus' explorations in the Americas; students can get an entirely different understanding of these events and their implications for society when viewed through multiple lenses.

Prejudice reduction encompasses the "characteristics of children's racial attitudes and strategies that can be used to help students develop more positive racial and ethnic attitudes" (Banks, 2019, p. 47). It is essential that teachers do not avoid topics surrounding race and racism in their classrooms and succumb to the feeling that it is inappropriate to bring up these issues with students, especially in elementary grades. There is, unfortunately, too much research that informs teachers of the fact that by the time students enter grades where teachers do feel they can address these topics, racial bias and stereotypical views have already been developed (and gone unchallenged) since preschool (Derman-Sparks, 1989). Not only that, but teachers also display their own racial bias against students (particularly Black), and it is reflected in higher suspension and discipline rates in those students (Young, 2016). Teachers must become equipped to discuss and eradicate such occurrences. Whether teachers are comfortable with it or not, race and racism are already permeating throughout schools. Teachers must become adequately equipped to deal with it. Teachers at all grade levels can help reduce the effects of these negative developing attitudes by helping students acquire positive attitudes towards racial differences (Banks, 2019). Teachers can look at suggestions in chapter two on teachers reflecting on their racial biases and attitudes in order to help in this process. It was made clear that many well-meaning educators still cling to the ideology of color blindness in their defense of not needing to address racial bias (DiAngelo, 2018). Teachers need to continue to question the validity of this notion. When teachers cannot "see" the students that are in their classrooms, how can they be truly effective teachers for them?

Equity pedagogy encourages teachers to "use techniques and teaching methods that facilitate the academic achievement of students from diverse racial, ethnic, and social class groups" (Banks, 2019, p. 47). Teachers should be well-versed in the learning styles and characteristics that may be exhibited within diverse cultural groups. According to Gay (2010), learning styles are "the processes individuals *habitually* use for cognitive problem solving and for showing what they know and are capable of doing. They indicate preferences individuals have for perceiving and processing information, not the ability to learn the material" (p. 177). A key concept in understanding learning styles in equity pedagogy is that they are not fixed. Students can exhibit preferences for different learning styles for different learning activities. It is essential for educators not to stereotype students in understanding these preferences. Yes, researchers have found common characteristics such as African American and Latinx students preferring communal type learning experiences and should be provided with opportunities to engage in cooperative learning; just as some European American students may exhibit more individualistic tendencies due to their cultural value of competition. Some Chinese American and Japanese American students may fall into more than one category, as they have been characterized to value some communal and individualistic characteristics within learning as well (Gay, 2010). The best way to ensure all students are exposed to increased and equitable learning opportunities is to ensure students have a choice in deciding how to engage in the learning process (Borich, 2015). Teachers must be committed to differentiated instruction in the way students engage, process, and demonstrate their new learning.

The fifth and final dimension in Banks' (2019) multicultural framework is implementing an empowering school culture and social climate. This component most clearly reflects a school's ability to foster more equitable learning environments for all students. A few ways for schools to do this is to continue to assess teacher beliefs about teaching and teacher bias, assess school practices and policies such as tracking and evaluate disparities in Advanced Placement classes, achievement gaps, and discipline rates (Banks, 2019). The work needed to address and implement any changes needed to create more equitable outcomes may involve a complete reform of schools. In turn, resistance to the changes necessary for more equitable schools can be formidable. However, as Banks (2019) and other scholars in the field indicate, the benefits of the increased achievement in currently underachieving students and schools will be greater than any discomfort schools may experience in the process of reform.

Effective instructional practices are critical to the educational success of diverse students. Teachers invested in making sure their culturally and linguistically diverse students are receiving equal educational opportunities should heed the instruction of culturally responsive teaching practices and its promises for success. As student populations continue to grow and change, teaching practices should grow and change with students' needs as well. Every teacher has a responsibility to do everything in their power to ensure that they meet the needs of every learner. Whatever knowledge teachers lack due to the lack of exposure to diverse students' culture can be made up by adopting the methods that cultural responsiveness and multicultural education seek to convey. In today's increasingly diverse schools, teachers need to seek new and more informed methods of reaching and engaging their culturally and linguistically diverse students. All students should have the chance to see where their true abilities lie and be provided opportunity to embark on the journey that academic success can take them on.

AFTERWORD
EMBRACING THE CHALLENGE

"Precisely at the point when you begin to develop a conscience....You must find yourself at war with your society."

–James Baldwin

Being an advocate for misunderstood and otherwise misrepresented students in the educational system is not for the faint of heart. In a profession where the majority of the educators are from vastly different backgrounds than the students in their care, misunderstandings, and resistance to new ways of teaching are common. I am a witness to the resistance. However, the lack of understanding, denial, and resistance to how culture plays a vital role in providing high-quality learning experiences for all students can be detrimental. When well-intentioned teachers lack the tools necessary to help diverse students flourish, it can send students on a downward spiral of academic failure and disappointment. As classrooms become more diverse, the educational sector must equip all teachers with the techniques necessary to help nurture every student in their classroom. Becoming a teacher that is sensitive to the complex needs of their diverse students is essential. Promoting the promises of culturally responsive teaching practices and normalizing its implementation in schools are passions that run deep in my heart. I want to continue the pursuit to put an end to the negative statistics facing culturally and linguistically diverse students in educational settings. I want to help teachers replace archaic teaching practices that stem from outdated traditions, fear, ignorance, and bias with more inclusive practices rooted in empathy, compassion, empowerment, understanding, acceptance, truth and love.

I hope that this book will influence teachers to adopt more culturally responsive teaching practices. Once teachers can get on the same page, they can continue this mission with as much wisdom, passion, power, and patience that current scholars have already put forth. Every student deserves the opportunity to feel welcomed, valued, and inspired by their educational experiences. The current and constant rates of underachievement can become a thing of the past as education reform finally decides to move in the direction that best fits the needs of all students, not just the ones society has stamped as worthy.

Today's teachers are the educator's students are counting on. I encourage teachers to take all that has been brought to their attention throughout this book and run with it! Run with it back to their classrooms and truly uplift and empower students to make the world a better place. This road is rough, and teachers may journey it alone. However, take comfort in knowing that this journey has been undertaken by many before, and they have seen its rewards. Teachers should gather all the strength, faith, and determination at their disposal and put it towards this endeavor. It is the only way to finally eradicate the inequitable practices that continue to plague schools, and finally replace them with ones that seek to educate, empower, and embrace every student. No matter what teachers believe or whom they believe in, I hope we can all come to an agreement that Dr. King's words are infamously true, "a threat to justice anywhere is a threat to justice everywhere" (King, 1963). I hope that we will put compassion and empathy for students first, and defensiveness over perceived attacks to one's moral character aside. I look forward to the day when if teachers are confronted with the hurt that their words, actions, and inaction have caused another, it will be met with a determination for understanding and not a wallow in their feelings. I hope that teachers will no longer hide behind the fear of "saying the wrong thing" and just embrace that it will happen because no teacher is perfect. Just remember that those mistakes are only evidence that one is trying. Press on. The more teachers try to become a conscious educator, the more those mistakes will weed themselves out. For those true educators, I know the process has already begun and will continue throughout their lives.

For those still not convinced that discussions surrounding race and racism are appropriate for the classroom, I offer a truce. I did not write this book with the expectation that everyone would magically read these well-thought-out, personally experienced and researched words, make a total transformation, hold hands, and sing "Kumbaya." That's not realistic. However, I do hope teachers will at least understand that not everyone has to agree on everything, but that they can at least come to an understanding surrounding the different experiences students have had in the educational system based on their race, class, gender, religion, sexual orientation, ableness, or exceptionality and that those experiences are valid in all their variances and degrees. They are especially valid and essential to our students. Every student wants to be heard; every student wants to feel valuable; every student wants to be loved. If teachers can remember these things, they may be able to take the next complaint from a student about mistreatment as a call to be heard, a call to be valuable, a call to be loved. I hope we can begin to respond to these calls with an open ear to listen.

I look forward to finally reaching that mountain top where race no longer matters, and all people are truly treated equally, but we are not there yet. I hope that all educators, administrators, school board members, superintendents, and the like will heed the cautions addressed in this book. I hope that once teachers understand what it takes to truly educate ALL students, they can begin the work to make educational experiences more positive for all students. In turn, these students who have grown up in an educational environment dedicated to the focus on equity and justice for all will avoid repeating the mistakes of the past and begin creating future firsts for generations to come.

For educators, developing a critical consciousness is a journey, not a task, strategy, or quick-fix teaching fad. Developing a critical consciousness in educators is like planting a seed. In order for the seed to grow, one must take deliberate effort to cultivate it by continuing to immerse it in all it needs to develop. Teachers must continue growing in their understandings of the issues diverse students face. They must continue to seek out researched-based and best practices for every student. They must not become so consumed with tradition and conformity that they lose out on the promises of what new ways of thinking, knowing, and being can bring. Please take this seed of consciousness and plant it in soil fertile with love, compassion, empathy, and acceptance. Give it ample exposure to the light giving rays of truth and knowledge. Prune its sprouting leaves and figs with a critical approach to all that it is exposed to. Finally, give it time. Know that some stages of growth are quicker than others and some more painful to endure. But endure teachers must for the sake of the educational freedom to succeed for students. I encourage teachers to find someone to go along this journey with them, for it should not be undertaken alone. Even though every teacher has the capacity to plant these revolutionary seeds; it will be up to every conscious educator to grow the garden of change.

REFERENCES

Alexander, M. (2010, 2012). *The new jim crow: Mass incarceration in the age of colorblindness.* New York, NY: The New Press.

Anderson, M. (2016). "How the stress of racism affects learning." *The Atlantic.* Retrieved from: https://www.theatlantic.com/education/archive/2016/10/how-the-stress-of-racism-affects-learning/503567/.

Austrew, A. (2016). "Someone actually handcuffed a second grader for crying." *She Knows.* Retrieved from: https://www.sheknows.com/parenting/articles/1128338/7-year-old-gets-handcuffed-at-school/.

Banks, J.A. (2019). *An introduction to multicultural education.* (6th.ed.). New York, NY: Pearson.

Baker, A. (2019). "3 racial microaggressions teachers commit everyday-and how to avoid them." *Upworthy.* Retrieved from: https://www.upworthy.com/3-racial-microaggressions-that-teachers-commit-every-day-and-how-to-avoid-them.

Bear, C. (2008). "American Indian boarding schools haunt many." *NPR.* Retrieved from: https://www.npr.org/templates/story/story.php?storyId=16516865.

Benbow, C. (2018). "The gentrification of mlk: How America intentionally misrepresents our radical civil rights leader." *Essence.* Retrieved from: https://www.essence.com/news/martin-luther-king-jr-gentrified-whitewashed-american-racism/.

Bigelow and Peterson. (1998). *Rethinking columbus: The next 500 years.* Milwaukee, WI: Rethinking Schools.

Books, S. (2007). "Devastation and disregard: Reflections on katrina, child poverty, and educational opportunity." In Books, S. (Ed.), *Invisible children in society and its schools.* (pp.1-22). Mahwah, NJ: Lawrence Erlbaum.

Borich, G.D. (2015). *Observation skills for effective teaching: Research-based practices.* 7th Ed. Boulder, CO: Paradigm Publishers.

Brayboy, B.M.J. & Searle, K.A. (2007). "Thanksgiving and serial killers: Representations of American Indians in schools." In Books, S. (Ed.), *Invisible children in society and its schools.* (pp.173-192). Mahwah, NJ: Lawrence Erlbaum.

Brewster, J. & Stephenson, M. (2013). *American Promise.* United States: National Black Programming Consortium.

Brown, E. (2016). "Yale study suggests racial bias amongst preschool teachers." *The Washington Post.* Retrieved from: https://www.washingtonpost.com/news/education/wp/2016/09/27/yale-study-suggests-racial-bias-among-preschool-teachers/?utm_term=.9eaa00a05d8a.

Brownstein, R. (2015). "Report highlights racial disparities in school discipline-once again." *SPLC.* Retrieved from: https://www.splcenter.org/news/2015/09/04/report-highlights-racial-disparities-school-discipline-once-again.

CBS News.com Staff. (2002). "Ruby's bridge from child to adult." *CBSNews.* Retrieved from: https://www.cbsnews.com/news/rubys-bridge-from-child-to-adult/.

Chenoweth, K. (2009). *How it's being done: Urgent lessons from unexpected schools.* Cambridge, MA: Harvard Education Press.

Cherelus, G. (2019). "New jersey referee suspended after forcing black wrestler to have haircut." *Huffington Post.* Retrieved from: https://www.huffingtonpost.com/entry/new-jersey-referee-suspended-after-forcing-black-wrestler-to-have-haircut_us_5c1fe8cfe4b0407e907c38e8.

Collins, C. (2018). "What is white privilege, really?" *Teaching Tolerance,* 60, Retrieved from: https://www.tolerance.org/magazine/fall-2018/what-is-white-privilege-really.

Condne, J., Sanders-Weir, R. & James, S. (2018). *America to me.* United States: Kartemquin Films.

Darling-Hammond, L. (2010). *The flat world and education: How America's commitment to equity will determine our future.* New York, NY: Teachers College Press.

Dee, T.S. (2004). "The race connection." *Education Next*, 4. Retrieved from: https://www.educationnext.org/the-race-connection/.

Delpit, L. (2006). *Other people's Children: Cultural conflict in the classroom*. New York, NY: The New Press.

Derman-Sparks, L. (1989). *Anti-bias curriculum: Tools for empowering young children*. Washington, D.C. National Association for the Education of Young People.

Derman-Sparks, L. & Phillips, C.B. (1997). *Teaching/learning anti-racism: A developmental approach*. New York, NY: Teachers College Press.

De Villiers, M., and Sheila H. (2007). *Timbuktu: the Sahara's fabled city of gold*. New York, NY: Walker & Co.

DiAngelo, R. (2018). *White fragility: Why it's so hard for white people to talk about racism*. Boston, MA: Beacon Press.

Dweck, C. (2006). *Mindset: The new psychology of success*. New York, NY: Ballantine Books.

Eaton, S. (2007). *The children in room E4: American education on trial*. Chapel Hill, NC: Algonquin Books Of Chapel Hill.

Edney, H.T. (2006). *New 'doll' test produced ugly results*. Retrieved from: www.finalcall.com/artman/publish/National_News_2/New_doll_test_pro duces_ugly_results_2919.shtml.

Emdin, C. (2016). *For white folks who teach in the hood...and the rest of ya'll too: Reality pedagogy And urban education*. Boston, MA: Beacon Press.

Folley, A. (2019). "Majority-white school districts receive $23 billion more in funding than nonwhite Ones: Report." *The Hill*. Retrieved from: https://thehill.com/homenews/state-watch/431601-report-majority-white-school-districts-received-23-billion-more-in.

Freire, P. (1974). *Education for critical consciousness*. New York, NY: Bloomsbury Academic.

Gage, B. (2014). "The FBI vs. martin luther king: Inside j. edgar hoover's 'suicide letter' to civil rights leader." *Democracy Now*. Retrieved from: https://www.democracynow.org/2014/11/18/the_fbi_vs_martin_luther_ki ng.

Galster, G.C. (2012). "Urban opportunity structure and racial/ethnic polarization." In W.F. Tate (Ed.), *Research on schools, neighborhoods, and communities: Toward civic responsibility* (pp.47-66). Plymouth, UK: Rowman & Littlefield.

Gay, G. (2010). *Culturally responsive teaching: Theory, research, and practice.* New York, NY: Teachers College Press.

Givens, M.B. (2007). "Constructions of blackness: A white woman's study of whiteness and schooling." In Books, S. (Ed.), *Invisible children in society and its schools.* (pp.157-171). Mahwah, NJ: Lawrence Erlbaum.

Gorski, P. (2019). "Avoiding racial equity detours." *EdChange.* Retrieved from: www.edchange.org/publications/Avoiding-Racial-Equity-Detours-Gorski.pdf.

Guerrero, M. (2018). "10-year-old boy with autism restrained, handcuffed by school resource officer." *NBCDFW.com.* Retrieved from: https://www.nbcdfw.com/news/local/10-Year-Old-Boy-with-Autism-Restrained-Handcuffed-by-School-Resource-Officer-Parents-Demand-Outside-Investigation-490778451.html.

Harris, J. (2018). "Louisiana teacher makes racist facebook post." *Black America Web.* Retrieved from: https://blackamericaweb.com/2018/09/11/louisiana-teacher-makes-racist-facebook-post/.

Howard, G.R. (2016). *We can't teach what we don't know: White teachers, multiracial schools.* 3rd ed. New York, NY: Teachers College Press.

Howard, T.C. (2010). *Why race and culture matter in schools. Closing the achievement gap in America's classrooms.* New York, NY: Teachers College Press.

Johnson, O.D. (2012). "Toward a theory of place." In W.F. Tate (Ed.), *Research on schools, neighborhoods, and communities: Toward civic responsibility* (pp.29-46). Plymouth, UK: Rowman & Littlefield.

Joo, N., Reeves, R.V., & Rogrigue, E. (2016). "Asian American success and the pitfalls of generalization." *Brookings.* Retrieved from: https://www.brookings.edu/research/asian-american-success-and-the-pitfalls-of-generalization/.

KCAL/KCBS/CNN. (2019). "Teacher makes boy, 8, urinate in trashcan in front of class." KCAL/KCBS/CNN. Retrieved from: www.nbc12.com/2019/03/08/teacher-makes-boy-urinate-trashcan-front-class/?fbclid=IwAR27_nqucUKFJO3hc0QMjw4euIZmM3xm0X6bwjXNkS-SMq5z8A-RhVnOdiM.

Kendi, I.X. (2016). *Stamped from the beginning: The definitive history of racist ideas in America*. New York: NY: Nation Books.

Keneally, M. (2019). "Students from covington catholic high school, under fire over confrontation with native American protesters, head back to class." *ABC News*. Retrieved from: https://abcnews.go.com/US/students-covington-catholic-high-school-fire-confrontation-native/story?id=60568463.

King, L. (2015). Baby steps towards restorative justice. *Rethinking Schools*. (Vol. 29). 4. Retrieved from: https://rethinkingschools.org/articles/baby-steps-toward-restorative-justice.

Kiviat, B.J. (2000, April). "The social side of schooling." *Johns Hopkins Magazine*. Retrieved from: pages.jh.edu/jhumag/0400web/18.html.

Koppelman, K.L. (2017). *Understanding human differences*. Boston, MA: Pearson.

Ladson-Billings, G. (2006). "From the achievement gap to the education debt: Understanding achievement in u.s. schools." *Educational Researcher*, 35 (7), pp. 3-12.

Ladson-Billings, G. (2009). *The dreamkeepers: Successful teachers of African American children*. San Francisco, CA: Jossey-Bass.

Lew, J. (2007). "Korean American high school dropouts: A case study of their experiences and negotiations of schooling, family, and communities." In Books, S. (Ed.), *Invisible children in society and its schools.* (pp.103-116). Mahwah, NJ: Lawrence Erlbaum.

Loewen, J. (2007). *Lies my teacher told me: Everything your American history textbook got wrong.* New York, NY: Touchstone.

Loewen, J. (2011). "Getting the civil war right." *Teaching Tolerance*, 40. Retrieved from: https://www.tolerance.org/magazine/fall-2011/getting-the-civil-war-right.

Logan, J.R. & Oakley, D. (2012). "Schools matter: Segregation, unequal educational opportunities, and the achievement Gap in the boston region." In William F. Tate IV (Ed.), *Research on schools, neighborhoods, and communities* (pp. 103-123). Lanham, MD: Rowman & Littlefield Publishers, Inc.

Martinovich, M. (2017). "Significant racial and ethnic disparities still exist, according to stanford report." *Stanford News*. Retrieved from: https://news.stanford.edu/2017/06/16/report-finds-significant-racial-ethnic-disparities/.

McIntosh, P. (1989). *White privilege: Unpacking the invisible knapsack.* Retrieved from: https://www.nationalseedproject.org/white-privilege-unpacking-the-invisible-knapsack.

McKee, C. (2018). "Students, parents speak out against cibola high teacher racism incident." *KREQ*. Retrieved from: https://www.krqe.com/news/albuquerque-metro/students-parents-speak-out-against-cibola-high-teacher-racism-incident/1626212604?fbclid=IwAR2QxCMmQPiosJhb_WVNMjujTQsLsScSbzcc1pIr6qW8OOAwLzCC82U6Qqo.

Meltzer, M. (1972). *Slavery: From the rise of western civilization to today.* New York, NY: Dell Publishing Co.

Miller, C.C. (2018). "Does teacher diversity matter in student learning?" *The New York Times*. Retrieved from: https://www.nytimes.com/2018/09/10/upshot/teacher-diversity-effect-students-learning.html.

Morrison, L. (2019). "Watch your tone, fix your face, and other unspoken rules for educators of color." *The Educator's Room*. Retrieved from: https://theeducatorsroom.com/opinionwatch-your-tone-fix-your-face-and-other-unspoken-rules-for-educators-of-color/?fbclid=IwAR1752eFPYZ50wqj8eExiXtwFeYNh61g6HJPnn9VSj8Ye5-iNIedQFHOR2c.

Mosenbergen, D. (2018). "Texas students will soon learn that slavery played 'central role' in sparking civil war." *Huffington Post*. Retrieved from: https://www.huffingtonpost.com/entry/texas-civil-war-slavery-education-curriculum_us_5bf6772be4b03b230f9ec629.

NAACP Legal Defense Fund. *Brown at 60: The doll test*. Retrieved from: www.naacpldf.org/brown-at-60-the-doll-test.

National Center for Education Statistics. (2015). *Selected Findings from PISA 2015*. Retrieved from: http://www.nces.ed.gov/surveys/pisa/pisa2015/pisa2015highlights_1.asp.

National Center for Education Statistics. (2017). *Status and trends in the education of racial and ethnic Groups 2017*. Retrieved from: https://nces.ed.gov/pubs2017/2017051.pdf.

National Museum of the American Indian. (2016). *Nation to nation: Treaties between the united states and American Indian nations*. Retrieved from: https://americanindian.si.edu/static/nationtonation/.

Ortiz, Paul. (2018). *An African American and Latin history of the united states*. Boston, MA: Beacon Press.

Osborne, M. (2018). "School superintendent resigns after making racist comment about texas quarterback deshaun watson." *ABC News*. Retrieved from: https://abcnews.go.com/US/school-superintendent-resigns-making-racist-comment-texans-quarterback/story?id=58019974.

Pang, V. (2018). *Diversity and equity in the classroom.* Boston, MA: Cengage Learning.

Prager, K. (2011). Positioning young black boys for educational success. *Policy Evaluation and Research Center*, 19(3), 1-15.

Raudenbush, S.W. (2012). "Can school improvement reduce racial inequality?" In W.F. Tate (Ed.), *Research on schools, neighborhoods, and communities: Toward civic responsibility* (pp.233-248). Plymouth, UK: Rowman & Littlefield.

Resmovlts, J. (2014). "American schools are still racist, government report finds." *HuffPost*. Retrieved from: https://www.huffingtonpost.com/2014/03/21/schools-discrimination_n_5002954.html.

Rivikin, S. (2016). "Desegregation since the coleman report." *Education Next*, 16(2). Retrieved from: https://www.educationnext.org/desegregation-since-the-coleman-report-racial-composition-student-learning/.

Romo, V. (2018). "Linda brown, who was at the center of brown v. board of education, dies." *NPR*. Retrieved from: https://www.npr.org/sections/thetwo-way/2018/03/26/597154953/linda-brown-who-was-at-center-of-brown-v-board-of-education-dies.

Rosario, B. (2019). "White teachers three times more negative with black students, rutger study finds." *The Daily Targum*. Retrieved from: www.dailytargum.com/article/2019/02/white-teachers-three-times-more-negative-with-black-students-rutgers-study-finds.

Ross, L. (2016). "Blackface on college campuses isn't about free speech; it's about white supremacy." *The Root*. Retrieved from: https://www.theroot.com/blackface-on-college-campuses-isnt-about-freedom-of-spe-1790857482.

Rothstein, R. (2017). *The color of law: A forgotten history of how our government segregated America*. New York, NY: Liveright Publishing Corporation.

Rudd, T. (2014). Racial disproportionality in school discipline. *Kirwan Institute for the Study of Race and Ethnicity*. Retrieved from: http://kirwaninstitute.osu.edu/racial-disproportionality-in-school-discipline-implicit-bias-is-heavily-implicated/?fbclid=IwAR3NFWXIprmKqMZWcwF3DsZu3fzxYOl-waSFB6yfxrBiYRpIbAejbo5SG_s.

Rury, J.L. (2005). "The changing social contours of urban education." In Rury, J.L. (Ed.). *Urban education in the united states: A historical reader.* (pp. 1-12). New York, NY: Palgrave Macmillan.

Safir, S. (2016). "5 keys to challenging implicit bias." *Edutopia*. Retrieved from: https://www.edutopia.org/blog/keys-to-challenging-implicit-bias-shane-safir.

Sampson, R.J. (2012). "Neighborhood inequality, violence, and the social infrastructure of the American city." In W.F. Tate (Ed.), *Research on schools, neighborhoods, and communities: Toward civic responsibility* (pp.11-28). Plymouth, UK: Rowman & Littlefield.

Scruggs, A.O.E. (2009). "Colorblindness: The new racism?" *Teaching Tolerance*. (36), Retrieved from: https://www.tolerance.org/magazine/fall-2009/colorblindness-the-new-racism.

Slattery, P. (2013). *Curriculum development in the postmodern era.* (3rd ed.). New York, NY: Routledge.

Sleeter, C. E., & Carmona, J.F. (2017). *Un-standardizing the curriculum: Multicultural teaching in the standards-based classroom.* (2nd ed.) New York, NY: Teachers College Press.

Smith, G.P. (1998). *Common sense about uncommon knowledge: The knowledge bases for diversity.* Washington, D.C.: American Association of Colleges for Teacher Education.

Sussman, R.W. (2014). *The myth of race: The troubling persistence of an unscientific idea.* Cambridge, MA: Harvard University Press.

Swanson, J. D. (2016). "Drawing upon lessons learned: Effective curriculum and instruction for culturally and linguistically diverse gifted learners." *Gifted child quarterly.* 60, 3, 172-191.

Takaki, R. (2008). *A different mirror: A history of multicultural America.* New York, NY: Bay Back Books.

Tatum, B.D., (1997). *Why are all the black kids sitting together in the cafeteria? And other conversations about race.* New York, NY: Basic Books.

The Associated Press. (2016). "Deputy who tossed a s.c. high school student won't be charged." *The New York Times.* Retrieved from: https://www.nytimes.com/2016/09/03/afternoonupdate/deputy-who-tossed-a-sc-high-school-student-wont-be-charged.html.

The Guardian. (2014). "US teachers are not nearly as diverse as their students, new studies say." *The Guardian.* Retrieved from: https://www.theguardian.com/world/2014/may/05/us-teachers-diverse-students-new-studies.

Tutwiler, S.W. (2007). "How schools fail African American boys." In Books, S. (Ed.), *Invisible children in society and its schools.* (pp.141-156). Mahwah, NJ: Lawrence Erlbaum.

Valencia, R. (2010). *Dismantling contemporary deficit thinking: Educational thought and practice.* New York, NY: Routledge.

Vaglanos, A. (2018). "Idaho elementary teachers dressed up as Mexicans and the border wall for Halloween." *HuffPost.* Retrieved from: https://www.huffingtonpost.com/entry/idaho-elementary-school-border-wall-halloween_us_5bdc725be4b04367a87c358d.

Wang, A.B. (2018). "A teacher called a native American teen a 'bloody indian' and cut another's braid, students say." *The Washington Post.* Retrieved from: https://www.washingtonpost.com/education/2018/12/04/teacher-called-native-american-teen-bloody-indian-cut-anothers-braid-students-say/?utm_term=.5cb311ddf8bb.

Wang, F. (2019). "Miami student accused of cheating on sats after her score improved 330 points." *CBS Miami*. Retrieved from: https://miami.cbslocal.com/2019/01/02/miami-student-accused-cheating-sat/.

Wells, A. S., Ready, D., Duran, J., Grzesikowski, C., Hill, K., Roda, A., Warner, M., White, T. (2012). "Still separate, still unequal, but not always so 'suburban.'" In W.F. Tate (Ed.), *Research on schools, neighborhoods, and communities: Toward civic responsibility* (pp.125-149). Plymouth, UK: Rowman & Littlefield.

Wu, E. (2014). *The color of success: Asian Americans and the origins of the model minority*. Princeton, NJ: Princeton University Press.

Young, Y. (2016). "Teacher's implicit bias against students starts in preschool study finds." *The Guardian*. Retrieved from: https://www.theguardian.com/world/2016/oct/04/black-students-teachers-implicit-racial-bias-preschool-study?CMP=share_btn_fb.

Zinn, H. (2003). *A people's history of the united states*. New York, NY: HarperCollins Publishers.

ABOUT THE AUTHOR

Salandra Grice is a former educator and the founder of Conscious Education Consulting, LLC. Her company provides professional development in culturally responsive and equity-based teaching practices. Her mission is to help educators create equitable and positive learning experiences for every student through dynamic, interactive, and reflective professional development for teachers and schools.

Please send comments and requests for information on consulting, workshops, or speaking opportunities to conscioused18@gmail.com; or call (832) 356-9650. You may also visit the Conscious Education Consulting, LLC, website at www.consciousednow.com.

CPSIA information can be obtained
at www.ICGtesting.com
Printed in the USA
JSHW010938210819
1151JS00010B/27

9 781634 988513